ANTONY C. SUTTON, born in London in 1925, was educated at the universities of London, Gottingen and California. He was a Research Fellow at the Hoover Institution for War, Revolution and Peace at Stanford, California, from 1968 to 1973 and later an Economics Professor at California State University, Los Angeles. He is the author of 25 books, including the major three-volume study *Western Technology and Soviet Economic Development*. He died in 2002.

PUBLISHER'S NOTE

Wall Street and FDR was first published in 1975. Sadly, the author was not able to update it in his lifetime. It is reproduced here in its original form, as a classic study of the subject.

Wall Street and FDR

ANTONY C. SUTTON

CLAIRVIEW

Clairview Books
Hillside House, The Square
Forest Row, RH18 5ES

www.clairviewbooks.com

Published by Clairview 2013

First published in 1975 by Arlington House, New York

A catalogue record for this book is available from the British Library

ISBN 978 1 905570 71 3

Cover by Morgan Creative
Printed and bound by 4edge Limited, UK

CONTENTS

Preface

In a previous book, *Wall Street and the Bolshevik Revolution,* (Arlington House 1974), the association of Wall Street international bankers and the 1917 Bolshevik Revolution was traced in some detail. *Wall Street and FDR* is a sequel to this earlier volume. Bankers were also associated with Franklin Delano Roosevelt between 1917 and 1934, as well as with the promotion of Roosevelt's New Deal and the rise of corporate socialism in the United States.

The evidence, based largely on FDR's own papers, suggests that there is nothing inevitable about the march of socialism. Socialism is the most inefficient, and certainly the most inequitable, way to run a society ever conceived by man. It has come to the United States only because it is very much in the interest of the Wall Street financial establishment to attain a socialist society.

How this was brought about in the Roosevelt era is the story of this book.

ANTONY C. SUTTON

October 1974
  Cupertino, California

PART I

FRANKLIN DELANO ROOSEVELT
ON WALL STREET

CHAPTER 1

Roosevelts and Delanos

The real truth of the matter is, as you and I know, that a financial element in the larger centers has owned the Government ever since the days of Andrew Jackson—and I am not wholly excepting the Administration of W.W.° The country is going through a repetition of Jackson's fight with the Bank of the United States—only on a far bigger and broader basis.

President Franklin Delano Roosevelt to Col. Edward Mandell House, November 21, 1933, F.D.R.: His Personal Letters (New York: Duell, Sloan and Pearce 1950), p. 373.

This book[1] portrays Franklin Delano Roosevelt as a Wall Street financier who, during his first term as President of the United States, reflected the objectives of financial elements concentrated in the New York business establishment. Given the long historical association—since the late 18th century—of the Roosevelt and Delano families with New York finance and FDR's own career from 1921 to 1928 as banker and

---

°W.W. is Woodrow Wilson—editor's note.

1. A previous volume, Antony C. Sutton, *Wall Street and the Bolshevik Revolution,* (New Rochelle, N.Y., Arlington House, 1974), hereafter cited as Sutton, *Bolshevik Revolution,* explored the links between Wall Street financiers and the Bolshevik Revolution. In great part, allowing for deaths and new faces, this book focuses on the same segment of the New York financial establishment.

speculator at 120 Broadway and 55 Liberty Street, such a theme should not come as a surprise to the reader. On the other hand, FDR biographers Schlesinger, Davis, Freidel, and otherwise accurate Roosevelt commentators appear to avoid penetrating very far into the recorded and documented links between New York bankers and FDR. We intend to present the facts of the relationship, as recorded in FDR's letter files. These are new facts only in the sense that they have not previously been published; they are readily available in the archives for research, and consideration of this information suggests a reassessment of FDR's role in the history of the 20th century.

Perhaps it always makes good politics to appear before the American electorate as a critic, if not an outright enemy, of the international banking fraternity. Without question Franklin D. Roosevelt, his supporters, and biographers portray FDR as a knight in shining armor wielding the sword of righteous vengeance against the robber barons in the skyscrapers of downtown Manhattan. For instance, the Roosevelt Presidential campaign of 1932 consistently attacked President Herbert Hoover for his alleged association with international bankers and for pandering to the demands of big business. Witness the following FDR blast in the depths of the Great Depression at Hoover's public support for business and individualism, uttered in the campaign address in Columbus, Ohio, August 20, 1932:

> Appraising the situation in the bitter dawn of a cold morning after, what do we find? We find two thirds of American industry concentrated in a few hundred corporations and actually managed by not more than five human individuals.
> We find more than half of the savings of the country invested in corporate stocks and bonds, and made the sport of the American stock market.
> We find fewer than three dozen private banking houses, and stock selling adjuncts of commercial banks, directing the flow of American capital.
> In other words, we find concentrated economic power in a few hands, the precise opposite of the individualism of which the President speaks.[2]

This statement makes Franklin Delano Roosevelt appear as another Andrew Jackson, contesting a bankers' monopoly and their stranglehold on American industry. But was FDR also an unwilling (or possibly a willing) tool of the Wall Street bankers, as we could infer from his letter to Colonel Edward House, cited in the epigraph to this chapter? Clearly if, as Roosevelt wrote to House, a "financial element in the larger cities has owned the Government ever since the days of Andrew Jackson," then neither Hoover nor Roosevelt was being intellectually honest in his presentation of the issues to the American public. The gut

---

2. *The Public Papers and Addresses of Franklin D. Roosevelt,* Volume 1 (New York: Random House, 1938), p. 679.

issues presumably were the identity of this "financial element" and how and by what means it maintained its "ownership" of the U.S. Government.

Putting this intriguing question temporarily to one side, the pervasive historical image of FDR is one of a President fighting on behalf of the little guy, the man in the street, in the midst of unemployment and financial depression brought about by big business speculators allied with Wall Street. We shall find, on the contrary, that this image distorts the truth to the extent that it portrays FDR as an enemy of Wall Street; this is simply because most historians probing into Wall Street misdeeds have been reluctant to apply the same standards of probity to Franklin D. Roosevelt as to other political leaders. What is a sin for Herbert Hoover or even 1928 Democratic Presidential candidate Al Smith is presumed a virtue in the case of FDR. Take Ferdinand Lundberg in *The Rich and the Super–Rich.*[3] Lundberg also looks at Presidents and Wall Street and makes the following assertion:

> In 1928 Al Smith had his chief backing, financial and emotional, from fellow-Catholic John J. Raskob, prime minister of the Du Ponts. If Smith had won he would have been far less a Catholic than a Du Pont President. . . .[4]

Now the Du Ponts were indeed heavy, very heavy, contributors to the 1928 Al Smith Democratic Presidential campaign. These contributions are examined in detail in this volume in Chapter 8, "Wall Street Buys the New Deal," and no quarrel can be made with this assertion. Lundberg then moves on to consider Smith's opponent Herbert Hoover and writes:

> Hoover, the Republican, was a J. P. Morgan puppet; Smith his democratic opponent, was in the pocket of the Du Ponts, for whom J. P. Morgan & Company was the banker.

Lundberg omits the financial details, but the Du Ponts and Rockefellers are certainly on record in Congressional investigations as the largest contributors to the 1928 Hoover campaign. But Wall Street withdrew its support of Herbert Hoover in 1932 and switched to FDR. Lundberg omits to mention this critical and pivotal withdrawal. Why did Wall Street switch? Because, as we shall see later, Herbert Hoover would not adopt the Swope Plan created by Gerard Swope, long-time president of General Electric. By contrast, FDR accepted the plan, and it became FDR's National Industrial Recovery Act. So while Hoover was indebted to Wall Street, FDR was much more so.

Arthur M. Schlesinger Jr. in *The Crisis of the Old Order: 1919-1933*

3. New York: Lyle Stuart, 1968.
4. Ibid., p. 172.

comes closer to the point than any establishment historian, but like other Rooseveltophiles fails to carry the facts to their ultimate and logical conclusions. Schlesinger notes that after the 1928 election the Democratic Party had a debt of $1.6 million and "Two of the leading creditors, John J. Raskob and Bernard Baruch, were philanthropic Democratic millionaires, prepared to help carry the party along until 1932".[5] John J. Raskob was vice president of Du Pont and also of General Motors, the largest corporation in the United States. Bernard Baruch was by his own admissions at the very heart of Wall Street speculation. Schlesinger adds that, in return for Wall Street's benevolence, "they naturally expected influence in shaping the party's organization and policy."[6] Unfortunately, Arthur Schlesinger, who (unlike most Rooseveltian biographers) has his finger on the very pulse of the problem, drops the question to continue with a discussion of the superficialities of politics—conventions, politicians, political give-and-take, and the occasional clashes that mask the underlying realities. Obviously, the hand on the purse ultimately decrees which policies are implemented, when, and by whom.

A similar protective attitude for FDR may be found in the four-volume biography by Frank Freidel, *Franklin D. Roosevelt.*[7] Discussing the shattering failure of the Bank of the United States just before Christmas 1930, Freidel glosses over FDR's negligence while Governor of the State of New York. The Bank of the United States had 450,000 depositors, of which 400,000 accounts held less than $400. In other words, the Bank of the United States was a little man's bank. A report by Senator Robert Moses on the condition of an earlier banking failure—City Trust—had been ignored by Governor F. D. Roosevelt, who appointed another commission that produced milder recommendations for banking reform. Freidel poses the question:

> Why had he [FDR] failed to fight through reform legislation which would have prevented the Bank of the United States debacle? These are sharp questions that critics of Roosevelt asked at the time and later.[8]

Freidel concludes that the answer lies in FDR's "personal confi-

5. Boston: Riverside Press, 1957, p. 273.
6. Ibid.
7. This series is: Frank Freidel, *Franklin D. Roosevelt: The Apprenticeship.* (1952), hereafter cited as Freidel, *The Apprenticeship;* Freidel, *Franklin D. Roosevelt: The Ordeal* (1954), hereafter cited as Freidel, *The Ordeal;* Freidel, *Franklin D. Roosevelt: The Triumph* (1956), hereafter cited as Freidel, *The Triumph;* Freidel, *Franklin D. Roosevelt, Launching The New Deal* (1973). All four volumes published in Boston by Little, Brown.
8. Freidel, *The Triumph,* op. cit., p. 187.

dence in the banking community." Why did FDR have this complete confidence? Because, writes Freidel,

> Herbert Lehman was one of the soundest as well as politically the most liberal of Wall Street bankers; in banking matters Roosevelt seems to have followed Lehman's lead, and that was to cooperate as far as possible with the banking titans.[9]

This is something like saying that, if your banker is a liberal and loses your money, that's OK, because after all he *is* a liberal and a supporter of FDR. On the other hand, however, if your banker loses your money and happens *not* to be a liberal or a supporter of FDR, then he is a crook and must pay the price of his sins.

The four-volume Freidel biography has but a single chapter on FDR as "Businessman," the most space given by any major FDR biographer. Even Freidel reduces important ventures to a mere paragraph. For example, while the American Investigation Corporation venture is not named, an associated venture, General Air Service, is mentioned, but dismissed with a paragraph:

> In 1923, together with Owen D. Young, Benedict Crowell (who had been Assistant Secretary of War under Wilson), and other notables, he organized the General Air Service to operate helium-filled dirigibles between New York and Chicago.[10]

We shall see that there was a lot more to General Air Service (and more importantly the unmentioned American Investigation Corporation) than this paragraph indicates. In particular, exploration of the Freidel phrase "and other notables" suggests that FDR had entree to and worked in cooperation with some prominent Wall Street elements.

Why do Schlesinger, Freidel, and other lesser FDR biographers avoid the issue and show reluctance to pursue the leads? Simply because, when you probe the facts, Roosevelt was a creation of Wall Street, an integral part of the New York banking fraternity, and had the pecuniary interests of the financial establishment very much at heart.

When the information is laid out in detail, it is absurd to think that Wall Street would hesitate for a second to accept Roosevelt as a welcome candidate for President: he was one of their own, whereas businessman Herbert Hoover had worked abroad for 20 years before being recalled by Woodrow Wilson to take over the Food Administration in World War I.

To be specific, Franklin D. Roosevelt was, at one time or another during the 1920s, a vice president of the Fidelity & Deposit Company

9. Ibid., p. 188.
10. Freidel, *The Ordeal,* op. cit., p. 149.

(120 Broadway); the president of an industry trade association, the American Construction Council (28 West 44th Street); a partner in Roosevelt & O'Connor (120 Broadway); a partner in Marvin, Hooker & Roosevelt (52 Wall Street); the president of United European Investors, Ltd. (7 Pine Street); a director of International Germanic Trust, Inc. (in the Standard Oil Building at 26 Broadway); a director of Consolidated Automatic Merchandising Corporation, a paper organization; a trustee of Georgia Warm Springs Foundation (120 Broadway); a director of American Investigation Corporation (37-39 Pine Street); a director of Sanitary Postage Service Corporation (285 Madison Avenue); the chairman of the General Trust Company (15 Broad Street); a director of Photomaton (551 Fifth Avenue); a director of Mantacal Oil Corporation (Rock Springs, Wyoming); and an incorporator of the Federal International Investment Trust.

That's a pretty fair list of directorships. It surely earns FDR the title of Wall Streeter *par excellence*. Most who work on "the Street" never achieve, and probably never even dream about achieving, a record of 11 corporate directorships, two law partnerships, and the presidency of a major trade association.

In probing these directorships and their associated activities, we find that Roosevelt was a banker and a speculator, the two occupations he emphatically denounced in the 1932 Presidential election. Moreover, while banking and speculation have legitimate roles in a free society—indeed, they are essential for a sane monetary system—both can be abused. FDR's correspondence in the files deposited at the FDR Library in Hyde Park yields evidence—and evidence one reads with a heavy heart—that FDR was associated with the more unsavory elements of Wall Street banking and speculation, and one can arrive at no conclusion other than that FDR used the political arena, not the impartial market place, to make his profits.[11]

---

11. This raises a legitimate question concerning the scope of this book and the nature of the relevant evidence. The author is interested only in establishing the relationship between Wall Street and FDR and drawing conclusions from that relationship. Therefore, episodes that occurred in 1921, while FDR was on Wall Street, but not associated directly with his financial activities, are omitted. For example, in 1921 the Senate Naval Affairs Committee issued a report with 27 conclusions, almost all critical of FDR, and posing serious moral questions. The first conclusion in the Senate report reads:

"That immoral and lewd acts were practiced under instructions or suggestions, by a number of the enlisted personnel of the United States Navy, in and out of uniform, for the purpose of securing evidence against sexual perverts, and authorization for the use of these enlisted men as operators or detectives was given both orally and in writing to Lieut. Hudson by Assistant Secretary Franklin D. Roosevelt, with the knowledge and consent of Josephus Daniels, Secretary of the Navy."

So we shall find it not surprising that the Wall Street groups that supported Al Smith and Herbert Hoover, both with strong ties to the financial community, also supported Franklin D. Roosevelt. In fact, at the political crossroads in 1932, when the choice was between Herbert Hoover and FDR, Wall Street chose Roosevelt and dropped Hoover.

Given this information, how do we explain FDR's career on Wall Street? And his service to Wall Street in creating, in partnership with Herbert Hoover, the trade associations of the 1920s so earnestly sought by the banking fraternity? Or FDR's friendship with key Wall Street operators John Raskob and Barney Baruch? To place this in perspective we must go back in history and examine the background of the Roosevelt and Delano families, which have been associated with New York banking since the 18th century.

THE DELANO FAMILY AND WALL STREET

The Delano family proudly traces its ancestors back to the Actii, a 600 B.C. Roman family. They are equally proud of Franklin Delano Roosevelt. Indeed, the Delanos claim that the Delano influence was the predominant factor in FDR's life work and accounts for his extraordinary achievements. Be that as it may, there is no question that the Delano side of the family links FDR to many other rulers and other politicians. According to the Delano family history,[12] "Franklin shared common ancestry with one third of his predecessors in the White House." The Presidents linked to FDR on the Delano side are John Adams, James Madison, John Quincy Adams, William Henry Harrison, Zachary Taylor, Andrew Johnson, Ulysses S. Grant, Benjamin Harrison, and William Howard Taft. On the Roosevelt side of the family, FDR was related to Theodore Roosevelt and Martin Van Buren, who married Mary Aspinwall Roosevelt. The wife of George Washington, Martha Dandridge, was among FDR's ancestors, and it is claimed by Daniel

The 26 related conclusions and the minority report are contained in United States Senate, Committee on Naval Affairs, 67th Congress, 1st Session, *Alleged Immoral Conditions at Newport (R.I.) Naval Training Station* (Washington: Government Printing Office, 1921).

However, while FDR's conduct in the U.S. Navy may have been inexcusable and may or may not reflect on his moral fiber, such conduct is not pertinent to this book, and these incidents are omitted.

It should also be noted that, where FDR's correspondence is of critical import for the argument of this book, it is the practice to quote sections verbatim, without paraphrasing, to allow the reader to make his own interpretations.

12. Daniel W. Delano, Jr., *Franklin Roosevelt and the Delano Influence* (Pittsburgh, Pa.: Nudi Publications, 1946), p. 53.

Delano that Winston Churchill and Franklin D. Roosevelt were "eighth cousins, once removed."[13] This almost makes the United States a nation ruled by a royal family, a minimonarchy.

The reader must make his own judgment on Delano's genealogical claims; this author lacks the ability to analyze the confused and complex family relationships involved. More to the point and without question, the Delanos were active in Wall Street in the 1920s and 1930s and long before. The Delanos were prominent in railroad development in the United States and abroad. Lyman Delano (1883-1944) was a prominent railroad executive and maternal grandfather of Franklin D. Roosevelt. Like FDR, Lyman began his career in the insurance business, with the Northwestern Life Insurance of Chicago, followed by two years with Stone & Webster.[14] For most of his business life Lyman Delano served on the board of the Atlantic Coast Line Railroad, as president in 1920 and as chairman of the board from 1931 to 1940. Other important affiliations of Lyman Delano were director (along with W. Averell Harriman) of the Aviation Corporation, Pan American Airways, P & O Steamship Lines, and half a dozen railroad companies.

Another Wall Street Delano was Moreau Delano, a partner in Brown Brothers & Co. (after 1933 it absorbed Harriman & Co. to become Brown Brothers, Harriman) and a director of Cuban Cane Products Co. and the American Bank Note Company.

The really notable Delano on Wall Street was FDR's "favorite uncle" (according to Elliott Roosevelt), Frederic Adrian Delano (1863-1953), who started his career with the Chicago, Burlington and Quincy Railroad and later assumed the presidency of the Wheeling & Lake Erie Railroad, the Wabash Railroad, and in 1913 the Chicago, Indianapolis and Louisville Railway. "Uncle Fred" was consulted in 1921 at a critical point in FDR's infantile paralysis attack, quickly found Dr. Samuel A. Levine for an urgently needed diagnosis, and arranged for the special private train to transport FDR from Maine to New York as he began the long and arduous road to recovery.[15]

In 1914 Woodrow Wilson appointed Uncle Fred to be a member of the Federal Reserve Board. Intimate Delano connections with the international banking fraternity are exemplified by a confidential letter from central banker Benjamin Strong to Fred Delano requesting confidential FRB data:[16]

13. Ibid., p. 54.
14. See Sutton, *Bolshevik Revolution,* op. cit., pp. 128, 130-3, 136 on Stone & Webster.
15. Elliott Roosevelt and James Brough, *An Untold Story: The Roosevelts of Hyde Park* (New York: Putnam's, 1973), pp. 142, 147-8.
16. United States Senate, *Hearings before the Special Committee Investigating the Munitions Industry,* 74th Congress, Second Session, Part 25, "World War Financing and

December 11, 1916

My Dear Fred: Would it be possible for you to send me in strict confidence the figures obtained by the Comptroller as to holdings of foreign securities by national banks? I would be a good deal influenced in my opinion in regard the present situation if I could get hold of these figures, which would be treated with such confidence as you suggest.

If the time ever comes when you are able to slip away for a week or so for a bit of a change and rest, why not take a look at Denver and incidentally pay me a visit? There are a thousand things I would like to talk over with you.

Faithfully yours,

Benjamin Strong

Hon. F. A. Delano
Federal Reserve Board, Washington, D.C.

Following World War I Frederic Delano devoted himself to what is euphemistically known as public service, while continuing his business operations. In 1925 Delano was chairman of the League of Nations International Committee on opium production; in 1927 he was chairman of the Commission on Regional Planning in New York; he then became active in sponsoring the National Park Commission. In 1934 FDR named Uncle Fred Delano as chairman of the National Resources Planning Board. The Industrial Committee of the National Resources Planning Board, which presumably Frederic Delano had some hand in choosing, was a happy little coterie of socialist planners, including Laughlin Currie, Leon Henderson, Isador Lublin (prominent in the transfer of industrial technology to the USSR in the pre-Korean War era), and Mordecai Ezekiel. The advisor to the Board was Beardsley Ruml.

Then from 1931 to 1936, while involved in socialist planning schemes, Delano was also chairman of the board of the Federal Reserve Bank of Richmond, Virginia. In brief, Frederic Delano was simultaneously both capitalist and planner.

Delano left a few writings from which we can glean some concept of his political ideas. There we find support for the thesis that the greatest proponents of government regulation are the businessmen who are to be regulated, although Delano does warn that government ownership of railroads can be carried too far:

Government ownership of railroads is a bugaboo which, though often referred to, the public does not demand. If government ownership of railways comes, it will come because the owners of railways prefer it to government regulation, and it will be a sorry day for the republic when

United States Industrial Expansion 1914-1915, J. P. Morgan & Company" (Washington: Government Printing Office, 1937), p. 10174, Exhibit No. 3896.

regulation is carried to such an extreme that the owners of the railways are unwilling to accept any longer the responsibilities of management.[17]

However, in another book, written about 20 years later, Delano is much more receptive to government planning:

A big problem in planning is that of educating the people. If the public only realized that there can be social gains from directed effort, and that the time to accomplish most by planning comes before the need of making changes are manifested, the other problems of planning could be more easily solved.[18]

Further:

The above brief classification of the problem involved in planning serves as a basis for indicating the need for both direct and indirect social control. Very few people really know the best use of land for their own advantage, to say nothing of planning its use for the common good. Institutions have done a great deal in educating farmers how to plan individual farms, and yet many of the farms in this country are poorly organized.[19]

In brief, the Delano side of the family has undertaken capitalist enterprises and has Wall Street interests going well back into the 19th century. By the 1930s, however, Frederic Delano had abandoned capitalist initiative for socialist planning.

THE ROOSEVELT FAMILY AND WALL STREET

Franklin Delano Roosevelt was also descended on the Roosevelt side from one of the oldest banking families in the United States. FDR's great-grandfather James Roosevelt founded the Bank of New York in 1784 and was its president from 1786 to 1791. The investment banking firm of Roosevelt & Son of New York City was founded in 1797, and in the 1930s George E. Roosevelt, FDR's cousin, was the fifth member of the family in direct succession to head the firm. So the New York City banking roots of the Roosevelt family extend without interruption back into the late 18th century. In the industrial sphere James Roosevelt built the first American sugar refinery in New York City in the 1740s, and Roosevelts still had connections with Cuban sugar refining in the 1930s. FDR's father, also named James Roosevelt, was born at Hyde Park, New York in 1828 into this old and distinguished family. This

17. Frederic A. Delano, *Are Our Railroads Fairly Treated?* Address before the Economic Club of New York, April 29, 1913, p. 11.
18. Frederic A. Delano, *What About the Year 2000?* Joint Committee on Bases of Sound Land Policy, n.d., pp. 138-9.
19. Ibid., p. 141.

James Roosevelt graduated from Harvard Law School in 1851, became a director of the Consolidated Coal Company of Maryland and, like the Delanos in subsequent years was associated with the development of transportation, first as general manager of the Cumberland & Pennsylvania Railroad, and then as president of the Louisville, New Albany & Chicago Railroad, the Susquehanna Railroad Co., Champlain Transportation Co., Lake George Steamboat Co., and New York & Canada Railroad Co. James Roosevelt was also vice president and manager of the Delaware & Hudson Canal Co. and chairman of the Maritime Canal Company of Nicaragua, but most significantly was an organizer of the Southern Railway Security Company, established in 1871 and one of the first of the security holding companies formed to buy up and consolidate railroads. The Southern Railway Security Company was a consolidation or cartelization scheme similar in its monopolistic principle to the trade associations formed by Franklin D. Roosevelt in the 1920s and to the National Recovery Act, another cartelization scheme, of the New Deal. James Roosevelt's second wife was Sara, daughter of Warren Delano, and their son was Franklin Delano Roosevelt, later President of the United States.

Franklin was educated at Groton and Harvard, then went on to Columbia Law School. According to his son Elliott,[20] FDR "never graduated or took a degree, but he was able to pass his New York State bar examination."[21] FDR's first job was with the old established downtown law firm of Carter, Ledyard and Milburn, whose principal client was J. Pierpont Morgan, and in three years FDR worked his way up from minor legal research posts to the firm's municipal court and admiralty divisions. We should note in passing that, when FDR first went to Washington D.C. in 1916 to become Assistant Secretary of the Navy, it was Thomas W. Lamont—international banker and most influential of the Morgan partners—who leased the FDR home in New York.[22]

There were other Roosevelts on Wall Street. George Emlen Roosevelt (1887-1963) was a cousin of both Franklin and Theodore Roosevelt. In 1908, George Emlen became a member of the family banking firm Roosevelt & Son. In January 1934, after passage of FDR's Banking Act of 1933, the firm was split into three individual units: Roosevelt & Son, with which George Roosevelt remained as a senior partner, Dick & Merle-Smith, and Roosevelt & Weigold. George Emlen Roosevelt was a leading railroad financier, involved in no fewer than 14 railroad

20. Elliott Roosevelt, *An Untold Story*, op. cit., p. 43.
21. Ibid., p. 67.
22. See Sutton, *Bolshevik Revolution,* for numerous citations to Thomas Lamont's connections with the Bolshevik Revolution in 1917, while residing in FDR's leased house in New York.

reorganizations, as well as directorships in several important companies, including the Morgan-controlled Guaranty Trust Company,[23] the Chemical Bank, and the Bank for Savings in New York. The full list of George Emlen's directorships at 1930 requires six inches of small print in Poor's *Directory of Directors.*

Another Morgan-associated Roosevelt was Theodore Roosevelt, 26th President of the United States and the grandson of Cornelius Roosevelt, one of the founders of the Chemical National Bank. Like Clinton Roosevelt, whom we shall discuss later, Theodore served as a New York State Assemblyman from 1882-1884; he was appointed a member of the U.S. Civil Service Commission in 1889, Police Commissioner of New York City in 1895, and Assistant Secretary of the Navy in 1897; and was elected Vice President in 1900 to become President of the United States upon the assassination of President McKinley in 1901. Theodore Roosevelt was reelected President in 1904, to become founder of the Progressive Party, backed by J. P. Morgan money and influence, and so launched the United States on the road to the welfare state. The longest section of the platform of the Progressive Party was that devoted to "Business" and reads in part:

> We therefore demand a strong national regulation of interstate corporations. The corporation is an essential part of modern business. The concentration of modern business, in some degree, is both inevitable and necessary for national and international business efficiency.

The only really significant difference between this statement backed by Morgan money and the Marxian analysis is that Karl Marx thought of concentration of big business as inevitable rather than "necessary." Yet Roosevelt's Progressive Party plugging for business regulation was financed by Wall Street, including the Morgan-controlled International Harvester Corporation and J. P. Morgan partners. In Kolko's words:

> The party's financial records for 1912 list C. K. McCormick, Mr. and Mrs. Medill McCormick, Mrs. Katherine McCormick, Mrs. A. A. McCormick, Fred S. Oliver, and James H. Pierce. The largest donations for the Progressives, however, came from Munsey, Perkins, the Willard Straights of the Morgan Company, Douglas Robinson, W. E. Roosevelt, and Thomas Plant.[24]

There is, of course, a long Roosevelt political tradition, centered on the State of New York and the Federal government in Washington, that parallels this Wall Street tradition. Nicholas Roosevelt (1658-1742) was

---

23. It is important to note as we develop the story of FDR in Wall Street that Guaranty Trust is prominent in the earlier Sutton, *Bolshevik Revolution.*
24. Gabriel Kolko, *The Triumph of Conservatism* (London: Free Press, 1963), p. 202. Willard Straight was owner of *The New Republic.*

in 1700 a member of the New York State Assembly. Isaac Roosevelt (1726-1794) was a member of the New York Provincial Congress. James I. Roosevelt (1795-1875) was a member of the New York State Assembly in 1835 and 1840 and a member of the U.S. House of Representatives between 1841 and 1843. Clinton Roosevelt (1804-1898), the author of an 1841 economic program remarkably similar to Franklin Roosevelt's New Deal (see Chapter 6) was a member of the New York State Assembly in 1835. Robert Barnwell Roosevelt (1829-1906) was a member of the U.S. House of Representatives in 1871-73 and U.S. Minister to Holland 1888-1890. Then, of course, as we have noted, there was President Theodore Roosevelt. Franklin continued the Theodore Roosevelt political tradition as a New York State Senator (1910-1913), Assistant Secretary of the Navy (1913-1920), Governor of the State of New York (1928-1930), and then President (1933-1945).

While FDR was in office, other Roosevelts assumed minor offices. Theodore Roosevelt, Jr. (1887-1944) was a member of the New York State Assembly from 1919 to 1921 and then continued the virtual Roosevelt Navy monopoly as Assistant Secretary of the Navy from 1921 to 1924, Governor of Puerto Rico from 1922 to 1932, and Governor General of the Philippines from 1932 to 1933. Nicolas Roosevelt was Vice Governor of the Philippines in 1930. Other Roosevelts have continued this political tradition since the New Deal era.

An alliance of Wall Street and political office is implicit in this Roosevelt tradition. The policies implemented by the many Roosevelts have tended toward increased state intervention into business, desirable to some business elements, and therefore the Roosevelt search for political office can fairly be viewed as a self-seeking device. The euphemism of "public service" is a cover for utilizing the police power of the state for personal ends, a thesis we must investigate. If the Roosevelt tradition had been one of uncompromising *laissez-faire*, of getting the state *out* of business rather than encouraging intervention into economic activities, then our assessment would necessarily be quite different. However, from at least Clinton Roosevelt in 1841 to Franklin D. Roosevelt, the political power accumulated by the Roosevelt clan has been used on the side of regulating business in the interests of restricting competition, encouraging monopoly, and so bleeding the consumer in the interests of a financial élite. Further, we must consider the observation conveyed by Franklin D. Roosevelt to Edward House and cited in the epigraph to this chapter, that "a financial element in the large centers has owned the government ever since the days of Andrew Jackson." Consequently, it is pertinent to conclude this introductory chapter with the 1943 observations of William Allen White, an honest editor if ever there was one, who made one of the best literary critiques on this financial establishment in the context of World War II; this, it should be noted, was after ten years of FDR and at the peak of Roosevelt's political power:

One cannot move about Washington without bumping into the fact that we are running two wars—a foreign war and a domestic one.

The domestic war is in the various war boards. Every great commodity industry in this country is organized nationally and many of them, perhaps most of them are parts of great national organizations, cartels, agreements, which function on both sides of the battle front.

Here in Washington every industry is interested in saving its own self. It wants to come out of the war with a whole hide and with its organization unimpaired, legally or illegally.

One is surprised to find men representing great commodity trusts or agreements or syndicates planted in the various war boards. It is silly to say New Dealers run this show. It's run largely by absentee owners of amalgamated industrial wealth, men who either directly or through their employers control small minority blocks, closely organized, that manipulate the physical plants of these trusts.

For the most part these managerial magnates are decent, patriotic Americans. They have great talents. If you touch them in nine relations of life out of ten they are kindly, courteous, Christian gentlemen.

But in the tenth relation, where it touches their own organization, they are stark mad, ruthless, unchecked by God or man, paranoics, in fact, as evil in their design as Hitler.

They are determined to come out of this war victorious for their own stockholders—which is not surprising. It is understandable also for Hitler to desire to come out of this war at any cost victorious for the German people.

But this attitude of the men who control the great commodity industries, and who propose to run them according to their own judgment and their own morals, do not make a pretty picture for the welfare of the common man.

These international combinations of industrial capital are fierce troglodyte animals with tremendous power and no social brains. They hover like an old silurian reptile about our decent more or less Christian civilization—like great dragons in this modern day when dragons are supposed to be dead.[25]

25. Quoted from George Seldes, *One Thousand Americans* (New York: Boni & Gaer, 1947), pp. 149-150.

CHAPTER 2

Politics in the Bonding Business[1]

I am going to take advantage of our old friendship and ask you if you can
help me out any [sic] in an effort to get fidelity and contract bonds from
the powers that be in Brooklyn.
Franklin D. Roosevelt to Congressman J. A. Maher, March 2, 1922.

In early 1921 Franklin D. Roosevelt became vice president of the Fidelity & Deposit Company of Maryland and resident director of the
company's New York office at 120 Broadway. Fidelity & Deposit of
Maryland was an established insurance company specializing in the
bonding and surety policies required on government and corporate
contracts and a range of individual employments ranging from secretary of a trade union to employees of stock brokerage houses. In fact, a
potential for bonding business exists wherever a contractor or employee can violate a fiduciary trust or fail to complete a contract, as in
construction projects. In brief, bonding is a specialized field of insurance covering the risk of noncompliance. In 1921 Fidelity & Deposit
was the fourth largest such bonding house in the United States, but not

1. This chapter is based on the FDR papers at Hyde Park, New York: specifically
   Group 14, file entitled "Fidelity & Deposit Co. of Maryland, Correspondence of
   FDR as Vice President, 1921-1928."

27

to be confused with the Fidelity and *Casualty* Company of New York, another insurance company, which incidentally had W. Emlen Roosevelt, FDR's cousin, on its board of directors.

Why did Van-Lear Black, owner of *The Baltimore Sun* and board chairman of Fidelity & Deposit, hire insurance novice Franklin D. Roosevelt as vice president of the important New York office? Almost certainly he hired FDR because the bonding business is unusually dependent upon political influence. Reading through FDR's Fidelity & Deposit letter files from 1921 to 1928, we find that only rarely do price or service appear as competitive elements in bonding. The main competitive weapons are "Whom do you know?" and "What are your politics?" In other words, politics is a substitute for the market place. Politics was FDR's forte and Van-Lear Black knew his bonding world when he acquired FDR. It is important to note the political nature of the bonding business because FDR's biographers have, in some cases, suggested that FDR, a business novice, was relatively useless to Van-Lear Black. For example, Frank Freidel writes:

> Whether Van-Lear Black hired him because it was a smart business move or merely to collect a celebrity is impossible to determine. The worst Wall Streeters unfriendly to Roosevelt were able to charge was that the company wasted the twenty-five thousand dollars per year it paid him in salary.[2]

What then were the roles of politics and politicians in the bonding business in New York State in the 1920s?

POLITICIANS AS BOND WRITERS

The pervasive political nature of the bonding business is reflected in a contemporary, but anonymous, news clipping found in the FDR letter files and carefully marked by FDR himself. The clip refers to New York State government officials negotiating state contracts while at the same time acting as members of private bond-issuing firms selling security bonds to state contractors. The newspaper aptly headed the column "All Under One Roof" and reported that Daniel P. O'Connell, a member of the Albany bonding firm O'Connell Brothers & Corning and simultaneously in charge of the public affairs of the city and county of Albany, was endeavoring to exert a statewide influence over the issue of his bonds, to the dismay of competing bond writers:

2. Freidel, *The Ordeal*, op. cit., p. 138. Freidel is unfair to Roosevelt. No evidence is given of Wall Street criticism of the appointment. Criticism is unlikely—given the political nature of the business, that politics was FDR's strength, and the long Roosevelt tradition on "the Street."

Whereas, formerly Daniel P. has been somewhat busy going on the bonds of various and sundry constituents, hereafter he will do his utmost, it is said, to wish his bonds on other persons, especially contractors doing business with the city and county.

His advent into the bondwriting world has been about as welcome as a snowstorm would be to a blushing bride on a bright and sunny June morning. Local insurance men, Democrats as well as Republicans, it is said, who have been engaged in writing contractors' bonds for many years, resent Daniel P's coming into their field, while perhaps admiring his ambition and display of courage and all that sort of thing; and in state political circles it is said that Royal K. Fuller, state commissioner of the bureau of canals and waterways, is fearful that if Daniel P. succeeds in the local field [it will be] to his (Mr. Fuller's) detriment, or rather to the detriment of the bondwriting firm with which he is connected and for whose benefit, it is said, he uses the influence of his position.

Bond writer cum office holder O'Connell then wrote soliciting letters to all Albany city and county contractors to the effect that he was in the bonding business at the City Savings Bank Building, owned incidentally by Albany Mayor Hackett and which also happened to be the headquarters of the Albany county Democratic organization. O'Connell's letter to State contractors concluded with the appeal:

I would appreciate it if you will allow this office the opportunity of serving you. A telephone call or letter addressed to me at this office will receive prompt attention.

It is important to note this prevailing and apparently acceptable use of political office and influence to feather one's own nest. In the light of the evidence below, it suggests that FDR was merely following the contemporary mores of his environment. The use of politics to obtain bond business is reflected in the FDR letter files and essentially is the only way he obtained bonding business while vice president of Fidelity & Deposit Company. Of course, his letters soliciting business to the other Wall Street Roosevelts are entirely legitimate. We find for example, a letter to "Dear Cousin Emlen" (W. Emlen Roosevelt of Roosevelt & Son, 30 Pine Street) dated March 10, 1922 to inquire about obtaining the scheduled bond for the Buffalo, Rochester and Pittsburgh Railway Company, a bond then written by the competing National Surety Company. Emlen replied promptly on March 16 that he "was able to speak to the President about the matter." This must have stirred FDR's imagination because on March 16, 1922 he wrote to "Dear George" (George E. Roosevelt), also at Roosevelt & Son, inquiring about the blanket bond taken out by the firm itself for its own protection.

Trade unions were a special FDR target for business; as each union local secretary and treasurer is required to have a bond, this was a lucrative field. On December 13, 1921 general secretary treasurer E. C. Davison of the International Association of Machinists wrote FDR:

We are now carrying the bulk of our bonding business with your company, which we were influenced to do in a great measure by the fact of your connection with this concern.

Then on January 26, 1922 Joseph F. Valentine, president of the International Molder's Union of North America, wrote to FDR that he was most appreciative of all FDR's efforts for the union while acting as Assistant Secretary of the Navy and

I have a desire to give the Fidelity and Deposit Company of Maryland as much of our business as possible . . . as soon as our existing bonds have lapsed, it will be a personal pleasure to have your Company handle our business in the future.

Union officials in Washington and elsewhere were prompt to request their locals to divert business to their old friend FDR and away from other bonding companies. In turn, local union officials were prompt to report on their diverting actions, information in turn promptly conveyed to FDR. For example, the president of the International Association of Boilermakers wrote to Secretary Berres of the Metal Trades Department, A. F. of L., in Washington, D.C.:

. . . You may rest assured that anything that I can do to be of service to Mr. Roosevelt in his new position will be a pleasure on my part, and I am today writing Mr. Roosevelt.

Naturally FDR exploited his old political friends to the utmost and with a commendable attention to detail. In a sales pitch dated March 2, 1922 addressed to Congressman J. A. Maher, FDR wrote two letters, not one. The first letter read in part:

Howe [Louis Howe, FDR's right-hand man] told me of his conversation over the telephone with you and I am inclosing a more formal letter for exhibition purposes. This is a little friendly note lest you think I have suddenly grown formal since I have adopted Wall Street as my business address.
    Do come over and see me. I know it will do your soul good to hear the language which Brother Berres and various others connected with the Labor Bureau, are using in regard to the present administration in general and Congressmen in particular. If the Missus happens to be out of hearing when you arrive I will repeat some of the more quotable extracts.

FDR enclosed for Congressman Maher a more formal letter obviously to be shown around to Maher's friends stating precisely what it was he wanted: "fidelity and contracts bonds from the powers that be in Brooklyn:"

I am going to take advantage of our old friendship and ask you if you can help me out any in an effort to get fidelity and contract bonds from the powers that be in Brooklyn. There are a large number of bonds needed in connection with the city government work, besides the personal bonds which every city official has to give, and I am in hopes that some of my old friends will be willing to remember me. Unfortunately, I cannot take this matter up with them myself at the present time, but as all my friends are your friends I feel that if you have the time and inclination, you can be of real help to me. I assure you the favor will not soon be forgotten.

Later we shall see how successful this approach was for F & D.

POLITICAL INFLUENCE AND CONTRACT AWARDS

FDR's political contacts and influences were of course well known within Fidelity & Deposit, and he was repeatedly called upon by other members of the firm to use his political expertise and personal credit to generate bond business, even outside New York. This may be exemplified by a letter dated August 23, 1928 from F & D director F. A. Price, in charge of the Chicago office, about business from local Chicago politicians. Price wrote "Dear Franklin" with a message that, since the death of Chicago political leader George Brennan, several names had been proposed as leaders of the local Democratic Party machine. Brennan before his death requested that M. L. Igoe be his successor, Price writes FDR:

> You undoubtedly got in touch with him while at Houston and in the event you have a personal acquaintance with him, I would like to have you give me as strong a letter of introduction to him as possible.

Price noted that recently when in Baltimore he had discussions with F & D company president Charles Miller about "the thought of making some deal with the new democratic leader in Illinois. It is with this view in mind that I wish the letter of introduction." As machine politics in Chicago has been notorious for its low ethical standards, it requires little imagination to visualize the kind of deal Price was suggesting and which FDR used his name and influence to further.

That personal friendship alone was insufficient to get bonding business and that some variety of sweetener was used is brought out in a letter on the New York political situation dated September 23, 1925 from John Griffin, in charge of the New York office contract division, to "My Dear Mr. Roosevelt." It discusses the complex interconnections between New York political offices and the bond brokerage business. In part the letter reads:

> The big victory of Walker over Hylan will, of course, make a new set-up in the bond broker situation. Sinnott & Canty, from whom we were able to get some bonds in the early part of the Hylan Administration and in the latter part were not so much favored, will no doubt be out of it and either Charles F. Murphy, Jr., Hyman & McCall, Jim Hoey, or a man

31

named McLaughlin, a brother of the Banking Superintendent, will be the favored one. As I see it, our strongest connection will be through Al Smith into Charlie Murphy or McCall or McLaughlin as Hoey has his own Company—the Columbia Casualty Company. Perhaps Murphy receives from the National Surety Company, or the Company to whom he gives business now, a larger commission than we might be willing to give for his direct business, but a word into his ear through you and, of course, through the Governor and possibly Jimmie Walker, would at least put us under the most favored nation clause or [for] any division of these bonds as you know all of them must be divided between two or more companies.

I know all of these people pretty well and favorably, but mere personal friendship will not be sufficient.

A meticulous reading of this internal company letter suggests that kickbacks were the usual way to get bond business from New York government agencies; note the paragraph, "Perhaps Murphy receives from the National Surety Company, or the Company to whom he gives business now, a larger commission than we might be willing to give for his direct business." The concluding sentence, ". . . mere personal friendship will not be sufficient" has an ominuos ring.

Politicization of the surety business, so obvious in Chicago and New York, extended also to the Federal government contract arena in Washington D.C. On May 5, 1926 F & D second vice president F. A. Bach in Baltimore wrote FDR about a $1¼ million Veterans Bureau building projected for construction that spring:

Dear Franklin,
Among other projects of the Veterans Bureau this spring is one involving approximately a million and a quarter dollars at Bedford, Mass., and I am secretly hoping that through influence such as knowing Mrs. Rogers, Representative of Massachusetts, that we might have some chance of getting a piece of that business although, of course, the biggest project will be at North Port, Long Island.

Similarly, to a contact in a "firm holding Navy contracts" FDR wrote:

A casual reference in a letter from one of my old friends in the Navy Department to the award of some 8-inch gun forgings to your company, brought to my mind the very pleasant relations we held during my term as Assistant Secretary of the Navy, and I wondered if you would feel like letting my company write some of the contract bonds that you are obliged to give the government from time to time. I would like very much to have one of our representatives call.

Louis Howe, FDR's right-hand man, also worked at F & D offices, also actively solicited bonds, and was not at all backward about canvassing business. Howe's letter to Homer Ferguson of the Newport News Shipbuilding Company in December 1921 noted that the company had entered bids on construction of the vessel *Leviathan* and thanked Ferguson for the bond:

> If by any chance the fact that this was Mr. Roosevelt's company influenced you in making this award it would cheer Mr. Roosevelt tremendously if you could write him a little line to that effect.

These political methods of doing business are, of course, a long way from the competitive market place of the college textbooks. It would be naïve to think that political preference and personal friendship have no role, or only a minor role, in business relationships. In reviewing FDR's bond business, however, it is difficult to visualize another business in which politics plays such an all-encompassing role as it did in the bonding and surety business in the 1920s. The morality of kickbacks and of the use of political office to generate personal business is questionable, and the legality is definitely doubtful. Much less obvious is the consequent loss of economic efficiency and loss to society as a whole. If purchase and sale of such bonds is determined by price and past performance—and personal acquaintance can be a legitimate factor in judging past performance—then the market place will yield maximum economic benefits and efficiency for society. In a politicized business atmosphere these impartial competitive factors are eliminated, economic efficiency is foregone, and benefits are reduced. We have, in effect; a microcosm of a socialist economy in which all decisions are politicized to the detriment of society as a whole. In brief, FDR's bonding operations were to some degree antisocial.

Yet other letters in the Roosevelt files provide authentic glimpses into the back rooms of 1920 era politics, the wheeling and dealing that has so often degenerated into outright corruption. Witness an FDR letter dated July 11, 1928 to first vice president George L. Radcliffe in Baltimore relating to the manner in which John J. Raskob became Chairman of the Democratic National Committee. Raskob was vice president of Du Pont and of General Motors and consequently as much a member of the Wall Street establishment as could be found anywhere:

> At a meeting last night the Governor [Smith] definitely decided on John J. Raskob as Chairman of the National Committee. He said he wanted an organizer and a man who would bring the Democratic Party into favor with the business interests of the country. My first judgment is that it is a grave mistake as he is a Catholic; secondly, he is even wetter than Smith, seeking the repeal of the Eighteenth Amendment: and third, he is the head of the largest business organization in the world. I fear that it will permanently drive away a host of people in the south and west, and rural east who are not particularly favorable to Smith, but who up to today have been seeping back into the Party.

> I don't know Raskob very well, but expect to have a conference with him within a few days, and will mention among other things the possibility of V.L.B. [Van-Lear Black].

Later in this book we shall record the enormous funds poured into the Democratic Party by Raskob and the quid pro quo for big business: the New Deal and the National Recovery Administration (NRA).

On August 24, 1927 another letter to George Radcliffe outlined the manner in which the bonding industry could get together on behalf of James Beha, then Superintendent of Insurance in the State of New York. This quotation confirms the fact that "regulated" industries are no more than political devices to keep unwelcome competition at bay and that the regulators can be in the pockets and act on behalf of the supposedly regulated industry:

> Vic Cullen[3] and I have just had a talk in regard to Superintendent Beha. Vic says that he thinks there is some move on foot initiated by Joyce, to get Beha into the National in some capacity and Cullen makes what to me seems a most worthwhile suggestion. It is that Beha might become the head of the Surety Association. We all like Beha and trust him; he is a man of courage and independence, and I cannot think of any one better suited for the position. Of course, it would cost a high salary—my thought is $35,000 a year—but this divided up among all of the members, amounts to but a drop in the bucket.
>
> If you think well of this suggestion, Cullen and I both feel that you are the man, rather than either of us, to approach the heads of the American, U. S. F. & G. and one or two others in an informal and confidential way.

On the other hand, there were attempts in New York to eliminate abuses in the bonding business. One such effort was that by State Architect Sullivan W. Jones to eliminate a state requirement for bonds. Governor Al Smith was at first induced to extend his approval to the Jones plan. This brought a swift letter to FDR from R.H. Towner at 160 Broadway to the effect that the Jones Plan would be disastrous and (if) "Governor Smith (has gone) astray some of his friends ought to put him right." FDR's prompt reply to Towner was, "I hope to see the Governor in the next couple of weeks and will then talk to him like a Dutch uncle about Jones' plan." We read no more in the FDR files about abolishing compulsory surety bonds in the State of New York.

That F & D's office was hardnosed about its own interests is reflected even in relatively minor matters: for example, no New York business association was able to win F & D financial support. On August 5, 1926 a request from the Better Business Bureau of New York for a subscription evoked a cold response from F & D. FDR passed the letter to vice president Cullen to prepare a "suitable reply," and Cullen promptly

---

3. Cullen was Manager of the New York production office.

turned down the Better Business Bureau. This turn-down was supported by president Charles R. Miller in Baltimore, "I am not so keen on
making a contribution toward the Better Business Bureau at this
time. . . ." Then the Merchants Association of New York wrote FDR on
May 23, 1925 about membership of F & D in their association. Again
Cullen argued that "the Merchants Association is of absolutely no
benefit to us." No law requires membership in better business associations, but these brush-offs make suspect do-gooder social appeals from
these nonjoiners.

THE PAY-OFF FOR FIDELITY & DEPOSIT COMPANY

This brief review of Franklin D. Roosevelt's career from 1921 to 1928
as vice president of Fidelity & Deposit Company in New York suggests
the philosophical road Roosevelt followed for the next two decades.
The bonding business was pervasively political, and FDR in politics
was like a duck in water. Political contacts made during his service as
Assistant Secretary of the Navy were utilized to the full, new political
contacts, encouraged by the Baltimore management of F & D, were
made, and FDR had seven years to practice this art of politics in business. The results for F & D were exceptionally good. Business expanded, in some measure perhaps because almost all business expanded in
the 1920s, but almost certainly to a major extent because of FDR's
political activities. In the period January 1st, 1923 to January 1st, 1924
Fidelity & Deposit showed a gain of $3 million in the year and surged
into third place among the bonding companies, a good jump ahead of
U.S. Fidelity and Casualty Co., its displaced competitor. The figures
read:

Surety Company Bonds in the State of New York

	Jan. 1, 1923	Jan. 1, 1924	Gain/loss
Fidelity & Deposit Co.	$ 7,033,100	$10,184,600	+$3,151,500
National Surety Co.	$14,993,000	$15,677,550	+ 684,550
Fidelity and Casualty Co. of New York	$ 3,211,900	$ 3,215,150	+ 3,250
Aetna Casualty & Surety Co.	$ 5,517,200	$ 4,799,500	− 717,700
U.S. Fidelity & Casualty Co.	$ 8,064,500	$ 6,817,000	− 1,247,500
American Surety Co.	$13,263,125	$12,127,400	− 1,125,725

The Fidelity & Deposit office at 120 Broadway was FDR's base of
operations in the 1920s, but the bonding business, successful as it was,

35

was not FDR's only business activity. Other interesting endeavors will be explored in subsequent chapters. These seven years in a politically charged business atmosphere—a microcosm of a socialist society, because socialist societies are also politically run economies—were undoubtedly a determining influence in FDR's later approaches to solutions of national economic problems. This was FDR's first exposure to the business world. It was not an exposure to the competitive market elements of price and product quality; it was exposure to business on the basis of "Whom do you know?" and "What are your politics?"—ultimately the most inefficient and unprofitable bases possible for business enterprise.

CHAPTER 3

FDR: International Speculator

One of the most morale-damaging aspects of the inflation was the "sack of Germany" that occurred at the height of the [1923] inflation. Anyone who possessed dollars or sterling was king in Germany. A few American dollars would allow a man to live like a millionaire. Foreigners swarmed into the country, buying up family treasures, estates, jewelry and art works at unbelievable low prices.

Marjori Palmer, 1918-1923 German Hyperinflation, *(New York: Traders Press,* 1967)

Franklin D. Roosevelt was organizer and president of several speculative international financial enterprises linking Germany and the United States, and in particular one enterprise to profit from the ruinous German hyperinflation of 1922-23. In 1922 FDR became president and was one of the organizers of United European Investors, Ltd., with a Canadian charter, but based at 160 Broadway, New York. In 1927 FDR was also organizer of the International Germanic Trust Company, Inc. and the Federal International Investment Trust, which never got off the ground. By far the most important of these speculative enterprises in the world of international finance was United European Investors, Ltd., formed to accumulate German marks deposited in the United States and to reinvest these marks in Germany by purchasing property from destitute Germans. Fully to understand the scope and meaning of United European and to follow the activities of International Germanic Trust Company, we need to make a brief review of German financial conditions in the early 1920s.

THE GERMAN HYPERINFLATION OF 1922-23

Lionel Robbins, the prominent British economist, has described the German inflation of 1922-23:

> It was the most colossal thing of its kind in history: and next probably to the Great War itself, it must bear responsibility for many of the political and economic difficulties of our generation. It destroyed the wealth of the more solid elements of German society: and left behind a moral and economic disequilibrium, a breeding ground for the disasters which have followed. Hitler is the foster child of the inflation. . . .[1]

The Treaty of Versailles imposed a massive reparations burden upon a defeated Germany, a country already financially weak from fighting World War I with deficit spending and postwar territorial reduction, with consequently reduced natural resources. Reparations have an effect on the balance of payments similar to imports. They require either taxation or deficit spending to offset the drain. If the course of deficit spending is followed, the result will be inflationary, and this was the course followed in Germany.

Germany was obligated by the Allies to make recompense for all damage to private property, except in Russia and to pay all costs of Allied troops on German soil, but no maximum limit was set on the demands. Germany had forthwith to surrender 100 billion gold marks, with payments of one billion gold marks annually after 1921. The final payments plan worked out at the "London Ultimatum" in May 1921 reflected these harsh and impossible terms and so provided a clear incentive to inflate to remove the burden of direct payments.

What is extraordinary about the reparations program is the identity of the so-called experts engaged in making the reparations arrangements, incidentally creating the monetary and social chaos alluded to by Lionel Robbins. The 1923 Reparations Committee had as its U.S. members Brigadier General Charles G. Dawes and Owen D. Young of the General Electric Company.

---

1. Constantino Bresciani-Turroni, *The Economics of Inflation: a Study of Currency Depreciation in Post War Germany, 1914-1923* (London: Allen & Unwin, 1937), "Foreword," p. 5.

The 1928 Committee of Experts on the Young Plan comprised, on the American side, Owen D. Young and J.P. Morgan, with Thomas N. Perkins and Thomas W. Lamont as alternates. On the German side the members were Hjalmar Schacht and A. Voegler, with C. Melchior and L. Kastl as alternates.

In brief, the General Electric-Morgan elements prominent in the Bolshevik Revolution, and as we shall see also prominent in the New Deal, were the negotiators of a scheme generally regarded as one of the prime causes of World War II—and incidentally a scheme in which these same financiers, as well as Franklin Delano Roosevelt, were to profit.

It is also worthy of note that businessmen on the German side of the reparations negotiations were associated with the rise of National Socialism in Germany. Witness Hallgarten in his essay "Adolf Hitler and German Heavy Industry:"

> ... in November 1918 a group of the Reich's most prominent businessmen, comprising Stinnes, Albert Voegler (then director of the Gelsenkirchen Mining Co., Ltd.), Carl Friedrich von Siemens, Felix Deutsche (of German General Electric), Director Mankiewitz of the Deutsche Bank, and Director Salomonsohn, of the Diskontogesellschaft, financed the movement of a Hitler forerunner, one Dr. Eduard Stadtler, who demanded the establishment of a German National Socialist state....[2]

The pertinent point is that the Felix Deutsche mentioned was a director of German General Electric and the American reparations representatives included Owen D. Young of General Electric, while the Albert Voegler mentioned by Hallgarten was the German representative in the Young-Plan negotiations.

The depreciation of the German mark into worthless paper currency as a result of this reparations burden imposed by these men is illustrated in the following table:

The German Mark in Terms of[3]

Date	Foreign Exchange	German Wholesale Prices
	(1913=1.00)	
January 1913	1.0	1.0
January 1920	15.4	12.6
January 1921	15.4	14.4
January 1922	45.7	36.7
July 1922	117.0	101.0

2. George W. F. Hallgarten, *"Adolf Hitler and German Heavy Industry"* in *Journal of Economic History,* Summer 1952, p. 224.

3. **Source:** *Statistisches Jahrbuch für das Deutsche Reich.*

The inflation accelerated following the formation of United European Investors, Ltd., with Franklin D. Roosevelt as President and John von Berenberg Gossler as a member of the German advisory board:

January 1923	4,279.0	2,785.0
July 1923	84,150.0	74,787.0
August 1923	1,100,100.0	944,041.0

The inflation went entirely out of control following the dismissal of Chancellor Wilhelm Cuno, who returned as president of HAPAG, and codirectors John von Berenberg Gossler and Max Warburg:

September 1923	23,540,000.0	23,949,000.0
October 1923	6,014,300,000.0	7,095,500,000.0
November 1923	1,000,000,000,000.0	750,000,000,000.0

The policies that led to the ruinous German inflation were initiated under Chancellor Wilhelm Cuno, who was, immediately prior to becoming Chancellor, the president of Hamburg-America Line (HAPAG). Two of Cuno's codirectors at HAPAG were Max Warburg, Hamburg banker and brother of Paul Warburg, member of the Federal Reserve System Advisory Board in the United States, and John von Berenberg Gossler, a member of the German advisory board of Franklin D. Roosevelt's United European Investors, Ltd.

Cuno was dismissed as German Chancellor in August 1923, but it will be noted from the table that inflation was already out of hand, and in November of that year the mark had depreciated to zero. The point to be made is that Wilhelm Cuno was Chancellor in 1922-23, when the mark was rapidly depreciating, and that Cuno came from a business circle that was able and willing to take pecuniary and personal advantage of the German inflation.

This terrifying monetary inflation and the ultimate collapse of the German mark in 1923 ruined the German middle class and benefited three groups: a few German big businessmen, a few foreign businessmen who were in a position to gain advantage from the inflation, and the rising Hitler movement. As president of United European Investors, Ltd., Franklin D. Roosevelt was among those foreign businessmen who took advantage of Germany's misery for their own gain.

THE BACKGROUND OF WILLIAM SCHALL

Unfortunately, there is a deeper perspective to this question of what could be called an élitist group preying on the world's misfortune. In

40

the previous volume in this series, *Wall Street and the Bolshevik Revolution,* we identified personal links between Wall Street financiers and Bolshevik revolutionaries. Some of these same personal links can be extended to FDR and United European Investors. The precisely established links previously implicated the then German Ambassador to the United States, Count von Bernstorff, and his friend Adolph von Pavenstedt, senior partner in Amsinck & Co., who was "for many years a chief paymaster of the German spy system in this country."[4] Amsinck & Co. was controlled by the J.P. Morgan, John D. Rockefeller, and other New York financial interests through American International Corporation. With Guaranty Trust Company, the American International Corporation constituted the central points for financing German and Bolshevik espionage in the United States and North America during World War I. Adolph von Pavenstedt and Edmund Pavenstedt, the two Amsinck partners, were also members of another financial house, Müller, Schall & Company. And it is at Müller, Schall that in 1922 we find Franklin D. Roosevelt and his United European Investors, Ltd.

After the public disclosures in 1918 of the connection between Amsinck & Co. and German espionage, the German interests in Müller, Schall & Co. were represented by Edmund S. Payne, a New York attorney. Müller, Schall & Co. was formally liquidated, and a "new" firm—William Schall & Co.—took its place at the same address, 45 William Street, New York City. The new firm, formed in January 1918, included the two original partners, William Schall and Carl Müller, who were now joined by John Hanway of Harris, Forbes & Co., Frank M. Welty, vice president of the American Colonial Bank of Puerto Rico, and attorney Edmund S. Payne, a partner in the law firm of Rounds, Hatch, Dillingham & Debevoise, who represented the German interests of the former Müller, Schall & Co.

The Pavenstedts were also "heavily interested in Puerto Rican sugar properties and owned and controlled the Central Los Canos."[5] William Schall was president of the Colonial Bank of Puerto Rico and president of the South Puerto Rico Sugar Company. Similarly, the Roosevelt family had interests in the Caribbean sugar industry going back to the late 18th century, and George Emlen Roosevelt was in 1918 a director of Cuban Cane Products Co. in New York. It is therefore conceivable that through this common interest in Caribbean sugar the Pavenstedts and Roosevelts became known to each other. In any event, it was the Schall-Pavenstedt group, previously part of the German espionage op-

4. See Sutton, *Bolshevik Revolution,* op. cit., pp. 64-67, and Johann-Heinrich von Bernstorff, *My Three Years in America* (New York: Scribner's, 1920), p. 261.
5. Paul Haber, *The House of Roosevelt* (New York: Authors Publishing Co., 1936), p. 71.

eration in the United States, that in 1921-22 merged with Franklin D. Roosevelt and several dubious financial entrepreneurs to form United European Investors, Ltd. to profit from the crushing burden of German inflation.

UNITED EUROPEAN INVESTORS, LTD.

The original organizing group for United European Investors, Ltd. comprised the aforementioned William Schall and Franklin D. Roosevelt, joined by A. R. Roberts, Charles L. Gould, and Harvey Fisk & Sons. The 60,000 preferred shares issued were held by Harvey Fisk & Sons ($25,000), Franklin D. Roosevelt ($10,000) and Schall, Roberts, and Gould ($5,000 each). In brief, FDR was the largest individual preferred shareholder of the incorporating group.

United European Investors, Ltd. was granted an unusual Canadian charter that provided the company with unique powers, including the right to promote trade and commerce between Canada and any other country; to acquire title to property; underwrite or otherwise deal in bonds, stocks, and shares; act as brokers and agents; undertake all kinds of functions in regard to purchase, exchange, and transfer of stocks and shares; lend money; carry on any business, "manufacturing or otherwise;" and buy and sell property. In fact, on reading the charter, it is difficult to visualize any activity that could not be carried out under its numerous clauses.[6]

The capital stock was divided into two segments: Canadian $60,000 divided into 60,000 preference shares and 60,000 ordinary shares, denominated in 10,000 German marks. The objective of the company as noted in the contemporary press was to invest the many billions of German marks then held in the United States and Canada in German real property:

Once marks are invested in property in Germany, the funds should begin to earn money immediately and the funds cannot disappear, since they are represented by the ownership of tangible property, and the advantage may still be taken of a possible rise in exchange value. Compared with this, the holding of mark currency or drafts is a most hazardous operation and the funds are either idle or earning very little. Besides if the exchange quotation should approach the vanishing point, there would be nothing tangible left for the holders of marks or drafts. The capital of the company will be invested in improved real estate, mortgages, financing

6. The copy of the U.E.I. charter in FDR's files carries an amendment by A. B. Copp, Canadian Secretary of State, that prohibits building of railways and issue of paper money.

42

of goods in transit and participation in profitable industrial and commercial enterprises.[7]

Reference to the preceding table recording depreciation of the German mark (page 39) confirms the remarkable timeliness of United European Investors, Ltd. In July 1922 the mark, with 1913 as a base of 100, was at 117 in foreign exchange. This reflects a heavy rate of inflation of the mark, but nothing to distinguish it from inflation in many other countries. Yet the U.E.I. brochure specifically mentions the possibility of the mark's "approaching the vanishing point," which it did achieve a year later in November 1923.

The actual investment of U.E.I. was carried out in Germany by a German advisory board that occupied an office in Hamburg headed by Senator August Lattman, formerly a partner in G. Amsinck & Company of New York (see page 41). The second member of this German board was Senator John von Berenberg Gossler, head of the Hamburg banking firm Berenberg, Gossler & Co. Berenberg, Gossler was also a member of the management board of the Hamburg-America Line (HAPAG); other members were Wilhelm Cuno, at that time Chancellor of Germany and responsible for his country's economic policy, and Max Warburg, brother of Paul Warburg, member of the Federal Reserve Board in the United States.

In a letter dated November 11, 1922 to U.E.I., the German Advisory Board recorded its initial investments: "All the investments so far made are of first class industrial shares." However, the prospectus issued in the U.S. emphasized investment in real estate, and on this point the German board wrote:

> As to investing in mortgages we understand your point of view but shall eventually come back to the question in case we shall be able to offer you mortgages with a gold clause which might be possible, and would exclude any additional risk in case the mark should further decline.

There is no mention anywhere in the United European Investors file of the purchase of real property or any other of the tangibles mentioned in the company charter and the public announcements.

The investments made by the board during the next few years were stocks of German companies. Further, the investment prices were cited in an unusual manner, not in German marks or absolute figures of any kind, but as a percentage increase, presumably from a 1913 base, which enabled the German Board to write to New York, "the shares which you so far bought have risen considerably with the depreciation of the mark."

7. This is taken from a press release marked "From Hon. Franklin D. Roosevelt" in the FDR files.

These shares and the percentage increase cited included, for example:

Deutsche Maschinen A.G.	bought at 1350% now quoted 1805%
Allgemeine Elektricitäts Gesellschaft	bought at 740% now quoted 5000%
Nobel Dynamit	bought at 1119% now quoted 3975%

The German Board did not mention the fact that the depreciation of the mark in terms of the U.S. dollar had been greater than the advance in the prices of the shares they bought as quoted in German marks. In effect, the claims of rising share prices made were illusory. One earlier writer has described it this way: "untrue and pure bunco steering, evidently intended to gull other holders of German marks to invest them with a company that could perform such miracles."[8]

This was not, however, of concern to the New York board of directors. At the regular meeting of the board held January 15, 1923 Franklin D. Roosevelt called the meeting to order, and George W. Müller acted as secretary. It was then recorded that the mark value of the German stock investments so far made by the company was more or less 73 million marks, and this investment was currently quoted at 420 million marks.

There is an interesting letter in FDR's files from Professor Homer B. Vanderblue, Professor of Business Economics at Harvard University, asking for explanations about the U.E.I. investment program. The letter was addressed to FDR, as president of the company, but replied to by Edmund S. Paine, who stated that the original idea of investing in tangible property, such as real estate, had proven impracticable as it "would entail a very heavy overhead owing to the necessity of supervision and operation," and so it was decided to invest only in German stocks "representing the indirect ownership in tangible assets." Paine added that the theory justified itself to a "remarkable degree:"

> Taking as a test the first Mks 60,000,000 invested by the company, we find that the appreciation in price of the securities has somewhat exceeded the depreciation in the exchange value of the mark. In other words, the securities purchased could probably be sold today for a price in marks which would bring somewhat more in dollars than could have been secured by the holders of marks had they sold them at the time of the investment in spite of the fact that the value of their marks has gone down tremendously.

However, Paine to the contrary, a "Statement of Conditions as of

8. Haber, *The House of Roosevelt*, op. cit., pp. 81-2.

January 31st 1923" located in FDR's files records that the book value per share of common stock at that time was $2.62 per share, while the average book value at the time of investment was $2.64—in other words, a slight decline.

At the directors meeting of September 19, 1923 it was confirmed that the total dollar value of investments was about $120,000, and in May 1925 this was still approximately the amount recorded in the treasury. However, in the intervening years following stabilization of the mark, conditions improved and a statement dated May 12, 1926 shows a net worth of $147,098.07, with 17,275 shares outstanding, and then equal to $8.50 per share. On May 21st, 1926 the company offered to buy all stock offered within 90 days at $7.50 a share. In May 1926 FDR resigned as president and accepted the offer of $7.50 per unit for his 1005 common stock shares.

Did the American holders of German marks who invested in United European investors gain or lose on their investment? If we suppose they held their stock to 1926 and accepted the company offer at $7.50 per common share unit, then buying at the issue price of 10,000 German marks in September 1922 (the date offered) they would have lost considerably. In September 1922 the dollar-mark exchange rate was $1.00 to 764 German marks. Thus a 10,000 mark share would be equivalent to $13.00 per share, and a share held from 1922 to 1926 would have realized a loss of approximately $5.50 per share; on the other hand, a shareholder would have avoided total depreciation and a loss of all his funds from holding on.

INVESTIGATION OF UNITED EUROPEAN INVESTORS, LTD.

The Roberts-Gould element that joined FDR and Schall on the Board of U.E.I. had a poor reputation on "the Street". In fact, Roberts and Gould were under investigation for suspected criminal activities. In July 1922, when United European was in the early stages of incorporation, a Mr. Crary, an old-time investigator for Proudfoot's Mercantile Agency—the top ranking investigation agency used by prestigious Wall Street firms—approached FDR's secretary, Miss Le Hand. Crary conveyed to "Missy" information about what he termed a "band of crooks with offices at 7 Pine Street" and with a nameplate on the door inscribed "United European Investors, Ltd." Missy Le Hand carried the information to FDR's right-hand man Louis Howe, who in turn raised the problem with Schall's earlier partner Müller. From Müller and other sources, Howe learned that Roberts and Gould were a part of this alleged "band of crooks" who, according to Crary, were "engaged in all manner of disreputable promoting and . . . he is certain that they have as a member of their force an ex-convict under an assumed name with a most unsavory reputation."[9] When the name United European Investors, Ltd. was posted on their office door at 7 Pine Street, investigator Crary, who had been routinely watching the office for a year, began quietly probing Roberts and Gould. Although Roberts was never in the 7 Pine Street office, Crary found that Gould "had been in the habit of using that office for at least a year, and was considered one of their (i.e., the crooks') tried and true friends." Gould's association with "the crooks" made Crary suspicious because, while the Proudfoot Agency had previously given Gould "a clean enough record," it had also put him in "the professional promoter class."

Crary's investigation was undertaken on behalf of the owners of the building at 7 Pine Street, "who intend to dispossess the whole bunch in a short time." It was during the investigation that the Proudfoot Agency came upon a circular listing the name of Franklin D. Roosevelt as president of United European Investors, Ltd. and William Schall as its banker. The evidence unearthed by the Proudfoot Agency was substantiated to Louis Howe by a Mr. Hanway, a member of the stock brokerage firm of Harris, Forbes. Hanway said he had "been familiar with Mr. Gould's activities for a number of years, and that he so thoroughly distrusted him as to lead him to make every effort to prevent from meeting Schall originally."

Even further, the Proudfoot Agency suspected that Gould had attempted to acquire confidential information from them and that Gould was acting as "a spy for the crooks to find out what knowledge Proudfoot & Company had of their crooked deals."

All this information was duly reported by Howe in a letter ("Dear Boss") to FDR (July 29, 1922). Probably most businessmen faced with this caliber of partner would abandon any proposed operation such as United European Investors, but Howe's memorandum to FDR recommends nothing of the kind. It reads in part:

> My recommendations are as follows: That Gould and Roberts be directed to immediately find new offices, preferably in a church or some other respectable place. That we get rid of Roberts, who is a wild man on publicity anyway, and who has no important function in this game, and that closest watch be kept on Gould. If Mr. Crary actually turns up the circular I would tear off the roof over it and make sure that its use is stopped until we are ready to make a formal announcement. I think it would be wise to insist that during the summer I be made a member of

9. Information taken from letter Howe-FDR, June 29, 1922 in United European Investors, Ltd. files.

the Board of Directors, particularly as both Jenks and Rogers will be away most of the time and some one wants to watch every action taken.

In other words, Howe suggests that precautions against double-dealing will be sufficient and that the best way to do this is to put Louis Howe on the board of directors.

In any event, the enterprise went forward as planned; Roberts became Secretary of the U.E.I., and Gould, alleged spy for the crooks, retained his role as active promoter and continued to report periodically to FDR by letter on the progress of their fund-raising efforts. On July 20, before Howe reported to FDR the substance of the Proudfoot investigation, Gould had written FDR from the Southern Hotel, Baltimore about his talks with Edward Clark & Co., the Baltimore bankers, whose partner Herbert Clark had known FDR from their Harvard days. Then on August 13, 1923 Gould wrote FDR from the Canadian Club of New York to relay telegrams received from William Schall in Europe and concluded:

I was sorry to hear you were again under the weather. Probably too much overdoing, one must not try to go to (sic) fast after such an illness. In any case I hope to have the pleasure of seeing you before I return to Europe in early September.

There is no clue that FDR communicated in any way with Gould, and the next letter in the files is from Gould to FDR, dated September 14, 1923 and also written from the Canadian Club of New York. This letter criticized the "jealous bankers whose scheme we hurt, and whose plans were upset. Had we not issued today we would have failed."

Gould then concludes, "Thank you for the great & noble way you have stood behind us, and I personally feel it was your strong attitude which is making our project a complete success," adding that when he (Gould) called on the large banks and trust companies to present "their proposal" he found "On every hand your name [FDR] was applauded as being the master mind in securing the proper operation to aid the unfortunate American investor," and that if FDR could have heard these comments from "the largest financial houses" it would have given him "great satisfaction."

On the basis of these letters, we must conclude that FDR knowingly entered a business arrangement with persons whose reputation was, to say the least, dubious, and that this business arrangement was continued after evidence of impropriety was brought to FDR's attention by Missy Le Hand and Louis Howe.

There is only superficial evidence that the whole United European Investors operation was designed by Roosevelt. When Gould tells FDR that his "name was applauded as being the master mind," it is reasonable to assume that Gould was flattering Roosevelt for his own purposes. There is really no evidence either way in the files or elsewhere that Roosevelt's background and financial knowledge were sufficient to originate a plan as ingenious as U.E.I.

CHANCELLOR WILHELM CUNO AND HAPAG

The disastrous depreciation of the German mark that was the *raison d'être* of United European Investors was concentrated in the period mid-1922 to November 1923. The table indicates how inflation got completely out of hand after mid-1922. The German Chancellor between mid-1922 and August 1923 was Wilhelm Cuno (1876-1933). Cuno was originally a civil servant, always active in politics, and in November 1917 was elected a director of the Hamburg-America Line (HAPAG). When Ballin, the president of HAPAG, committed suicide in 1918, Cuno became its president. After May 10, 1921 Karl Wirth was German Chancellor, and Walter Rathenau, the president of German General Electric (A.E.G.), was Minister for Reparations. Then followed a series of dramatic events. The German Minister of Finance Matthias Erzberger was assassinated August 26, 1921. In January 1922 Rathenau became Foreign Minister and on June 24, 1922 was also assassinated. In October of 1922 Friedrich Ebert was Reich Chancellor and Wilhelm Cuno of HAPAG was appointed German Chancellor. The depreciation of the mark occurred under Cuno and culminated in the financial crisis and his dismissal in August 1923. Cuno returned to the presidency of the Hamburg-America Line. We might note in passing the prevalence of corporate presidents in contemporary politics: e.g., German General Electric's Rathenau and HAPAG's Cuno. Owen D. Young of General Electric in the U.S. was also creator of the Young Plan for German Reparations, and German General Electric (A.E.G.) president Rathenau was German Reparations Minister in 1922. These appointments are usually explained on the basis of "the best man for the job" but, given the evidence presented in the last chapter on politics in the bonding business, we can justifiably express skepticism about this explanation. It is much more likely that the Youngs, Cunos, Rathenaus—and the Roosevelts—were mixing business and politics for their own pecuniary gain. Unfortunately, while we must leave unanswered the key question of how far these elitist groups used the state apparatus for their own ends, it is clear that, when we probe the background of Wilhelm Cuno, we arrive back at Franklin D. Roosevelt and the formation of United European Investors, Ltd. Cuno, under whose auspices the great German inflation raged, was a director of the Hamburg-America Line; John von Berenberg Gossler, the United European

Investors adviser in Germany, was also a member of the board of that company. In sum, Cuno and Gossler were on the same board of directors at HAPAG. Cuno's policies were essentially responsible for the German inflation of 1922-23 while his codirector Gossler, in cooperation with Franklin D. Roosevelt, was making profit out of the very same inflation policies. It makes one ponder.

THE INTERNATIONAL GERMANIC TRUST COMPANY

The International Germanic Trust Company, founded in 1927, was prompted, according to its promoters, by a demand for American banking institutions in central Europe. Among the organizers of the trust as approved by the Banking Department of the State of New York were Franklin D. Roosevelt; Herman A. Metz, a director of I. G. Farben; James A. Beha, Superintendent of Insurance for the State of New York; and E. Roland Harriman of the international banking firm of W. A. Harriman & Co. The president of the associated International Germanic Company and chairman of the executive committee of the trust company was Harold G. Aron, who had had more than his share of law suits involving stock promotion. The main offices of the International Germanic Trust were on the ground floor of 26 Broadway, the Standard Oil Building in New York. The authorized capital consisted of 30,000 shares to provide a capital of $3 million and a surplus of $2 million. In its application to the banking department the company was represented by Senator Robert F. Wagner; although not listed among the organizers, FDR's old friend, James A. Beha, Superintendent of Insurance for the State of New York, became a member of the board of directors.

The objectives of the company as stated by its president, Harold G. Aron, were:

> There appears to be a real need for an institution of sufficient size and backing, to take the place of those institutions which existed before the war and were primarily concerned in financing commercial intercourse between America and the Central European business world. Through its incorporators the trust company will have and develop relations both with Americans of German descent throughout this country and with business and banking institutions in Germany. It is the intention of the company to stress particularly the development of its foreign and trust departments, and to provide an effective fiscal agency in the expected liquidation of German properties and trusts still in Government custody.
>
> The company will, from the outset, be assured the support of important organizations and societies in this country, and the small depositor both in and outside of New York City will be welcome. It will aim to distribute its shares widely and in comparatively small amounts. There will be no voting trust nor individual or group control.

49

Roosevelt was involved in the flotation of the proposed company. A telegram dated April 7, 1927 from Julian Gerrard, president of the trust company, to FDR requested him to telegraph Frank Warder, Superintendent of Banks in the State of New York, to the effect that he (Roosevelt) was interested in the trust company. It was anticipated that this intervention would clear the delay in granting the charter. Board meetings were held in the Standard Oil Building, in FDR's office, and in the Bankers Club, the latter both located at 120 Broadway. The first meeting of the organization committee was held at the Bankers Club Friday May 27, 1927; although FDR was unable to attend, he wrote Julian M. Gerrard, "What is the news of the trust company?" Again on August 15, 1927 FDR asked Gerrard, "How is the organization work proceeding and what is being done in regard to the stock subscriptions?"

A considerable part of the FDR letter files of this promotion consists of requests for employment, stock in the proposed company, or related favors. For example, the National Park Bank of New York wrote FDR July 26, 1927 that it was interested in the creation of the International Germanic Trust Company and would be pleased to "have one of our officers address that body, going into detail regarding our facilities." In other words, the National Park Bank was looking for deposit business. FDR promised to take up the matter with the organization committee of the new trust company. Then on August 12, 1927 Roosevelt's partner Basil O'Connor dropped him a note: "Dear Franklin, On the Germanic Bank, see if you can get me 100 shares." The stock issue itself was heavily oversubscribed. It was planned to issue 30,000 shares, but total requests by September 12 were in excess of 109,000 shares, and by September 20 applications exceeded 200,000 shares from approximately 1900 individuals. The trust notified FDR on October 3, 1927 that his allotment was 120 shares at $170 per share and must be taken up by October 5. The telegram added that the issue was heavily oversubscribed and quoted at 187 bid, 192 asked, which would give FDR a profit on an immediate resale. This telegram from Howe added, "Would like ten of your shares for Grace if you are willing."

FDR was duly elected a member of the board of directors and notified on November 4, 1927 that the first meeting of the board would be held Friday, November 11 at the Bankers Club at 120 Broadway. However, Basil O'Connor, Roosevelt's law partner, apparently had cold feet or received adverse information on the promotion because he wrote FDR on November 14:

> I don't know what our position now is in this matter but if it is as when I parted I feel very badly about it. The proposition has not helped us any (with) other banking connections on which I have been working on a year and frankly it has all the earmarks that Gerrard (sic) thinks he can "kid you."

O'Connor suggested that FDR should resign from the board because "heretofore I have been able to say we have no banking affiliations, that was wrong. I can't say that now." Apparently, FDR did not immediately take this advice, because on January 19, 1928 he was notified of reelection as director for the coming year, but in a letter dated January 27, 1928 FDR wrote Gerrard as follows:

Dear Julian,
The more I consider my directorship and the trust company and the International Germanic Company, the more I am inclined to feel that it is somewhat futile. I have already told you of my partner's and my feelings in regard to extraneous connections on the part of either of us which involve merely attending occasional meetings and nothing more. It is somewhat difficult of course for me to go to the meetings at 26 Broadway in view of the steps but, frankly, I feel that in retaining my directorship I am accomplishing little either for myself or for the Trust Company or the International Germanic Company.

Whereupon FDR offered his resignation. It is notable that the reasons for resigning were "I am accomplishing little either for myself or for the trust company." In view of the rather unsavory reputation of the promoters, this explanation is a little weak.

CHAPTER 4

FDR: Corporate Promoter

The meshes of our banking laws have been woven so loosely as to permit the escape of those meanest of all criminals who squander the funds of hundreds of small depositors in reckless speculation for private gain. The entire Banking Law is in need of revision and the Banking Department needs immediately far more adequate inspection facilities.
Franklin Delano Roosevelt, Annual Message to New York State Legislature, January 1, 1930.

Quite apart from floating speculative enterprises in the field of international finance, FDR was intimately involved in domestic flotations, at least one of which was of some substance. The most important of these ventures was organized by a prominent group including Owen D. Young of General Electric (the ever-present Young of the Young Plan for German reparations described in the last chapter) and S. Bertron of Bertron Griscom, investment bankers in New York. This syndicate created the American Investigation Corporation in 1921. In 1927 followed Photomaton, Inc. and in 1928 the Sanitary Postage Service Corporation. Then Roosevelt became a director of CAMCO, Consolidated Automatic Merchandising Corporation, but only briefly, resigning upon his election as Governor of the State of New York. As we read in the above epigraph, by 1930 FDR has had second thoughts about playing with other peoples' money.

AMERICAN INVESTIGATION CORPORATION

German scientists and engineers made an early and successful start in the use of lighter-than-air vehicles or airships for passenger and freight transportation. As early as 1910 Germany operated scheduled airship passenger services. Patents for airships were seized in World War I by the U.S. Government under the 1917 Trading with the Enemy Act, and after the war Germany was forbidden by the Reparations Commission to construct airships. This left the field open to American enterprise. The opportunities presented by German work and development restrictions in Germany were observed by a group of Wall Street financiers: S.R. Bertron of Bertron, Griscom & Co. (40 Wall Street) and not surprisingly, since he was intimately involved in German reparations, by Owen D. Young of General Electric (120 Broadway). This group was particularly interested in the profitable opportunities for development of airship transportation in the United States. On January 10, 1921, as FDR was unpacking his bags in the offices of the Fidelity & Deposit Company at 120 Broadway, he received a letter from Bertron which read in part:

> My dear Mr. Roosevelt:
> Representing the small group of prominent men here who are becoming greatly interested in the question of air transportation, I had a long conference with Army officials in Washington last week in regard to it. I am advised that you, as Assistant Secretary of the Navy, are very familiar with this subject and I should like immensely to discuss it with you. . . .

FDR and Bertron met to discuss air transportation over lunch at the Down Town Association. We can surmise that Bertron filled in Roosevelt on technical developments up to that time. We know from the files that there was also a meeting between Owen D. Young, S.R. Bertron, and engineer-attorney Fred S. Hardesty, representing the German patent holders, who had good connections in Washington where the seized patents were in the custody of the Alien Property Custodian and had yet to be released.

This second meeting yielded a preliminary compact dated January 19, 1921 known as the Hardesty-Owen-Bertron agreement that planned the road to development of commercial airship operations in the U.S. A syndicate was subsequently formed by Owen-Bertron to "investigate all phases of aerial navigation, legislation required and methods of fund raising." Hardesty and his associates turned over to the syndicate all their data and rights in exchange for a refund of their out-of-pocket expenses of $20,000 incurred to that date and an interest in the syndicate. FDR's role was that of fund raiser, using his numerous political contacts throughout the United States. On May 17, 1921

Bertron wrote FDR that he had been trying to raise funds from people in St. Louis, Cincinnati, and Chicago, while Stanley Fahnestock, a partner in his firm, had been making the rounds in California and Chicago. Lewis Stevenson, another syndicate member, was at work among his contacts in the mid-West. So Bertron appealed to FDR for a set of personal introductions to potential contributors:

> Stevenson is very anxious for you to give him a line to Edward Hurley, E. F. Carey and Charles Piez, all of whom you know. He would like a letter also to Edward Hines, R.P. Lamont, and H.C. Chatfield-Taylor. I am afraid this is a large order. Won't you do your best?

FDR acknowledged Bertron's request, to the effect that he was sending letters to Stevenson "introducing him to Edward Hurley and to Charles Piez and E.F. Carey. I am afraid I don't know the others." Charles Piez, president of Link-Belt Company in Chicago, excused himself from participation on the ground that ". . . I am practicing the most rigid economy, bending a deaf ear to the most inviting and alluring prospects," and citing the "deplorable shape" of the industry. (This plea of poverty was supported by Piez's letter to FDR, on old stock stationary, with the new address printed over the old one—hardly becoming a president of a major corporation such as Link-Belt Company). Edward N. Hurley wrote that he was "not very active in business," but when next in New York "I am going to make it a point to call on you and check up the past."

On June 1st, Lewis Stevenson reported to Roosevelt on his fund-raising progress in the mid-West. He confirmed the fact that Piez was short of funds and that Hurley wanted to talk later, but that Carey might have some interest:

> Charles Swift, Thomas Wilson, both packers, are now considering the proposition, as are Potter Palmer, Chauncey McCormick and a dozen others. Since securing Marshall Field I have added to our list C. Bai Lehme, a zinc smelter of very large means; Mr. Wrigley, junior member of the great chewing-gum firm; John D. Black, of Winston, Strawn & Shaw; B.M. Winston and Hampton Winston, of Winston & Company, and Lawrence Whiting, president of the new Boulevard Bridge Bank. Gradually I am getting together a desirable group but I must confess it is discouragingly slow and hard work. My experience has been I can convince an individual of the feasibility of this scheme but as soon as he discusses it with his friends, who know nothing whatever of the proposition, they develop a serious doubt in his mind which I have to combat all over again. As a result of my observation abroad I am firm in my belief it can be made a success.

Stevenson concluded by requesting a letter of introduction to prominent Chicago attorney Levy Meyer. It is clear that by the end of June 1921 Stevenson had induced a number of prominent Chicago citizens, including Marshall Field, Philip N. Wrigley, and Chauncey McCormick, to sign on the dotted line.

So far as FDR is concerned, his sales letters on this project would do credit to a professional salesman. Witness his letter to Colonel Robert R. McCormick, of the Chicago newspaper empire:

Dear Bert:
As you happen to be a progressively minded person I am asking Mr. Lewis G. Stevenson to have a talk with you about something which at first blush may seem a perfectly wild idea. However, it is really something very different and all I can tell you is that a good many of us here, such as Young of the General Electric Company, Bertron of Bertron Griscom & Co, and a number of other perfectly respectable citizens have shown enough interest to look into the question further. All of this relates to the establishment of commercial dirigible lines in the United States. . .

Similar letters went to Chauncey McCormick, Frank S. Peabody of Peabody Coal, and Julius Rosenwald of Sears, Roebuck. These initiatives were followed up with personal dinners. For example, on April 21, 1921 FDR wrote to Frank Peabody:

. . . is there any possibility you may be able to dine with Mr. Bertron, Mr. Snowden Fahnestock and several others of us at the Union Club next Monday evening at 7:30? Bertron is just back from the other side and has some very interesting data in regard to these commercial dirigibles, which have proved successful in Germany.

FDR added that the group "will promise not to hold you up against your will." To which a reluctant Peabody telegraphed, "Impossible to be there, would not be at all afraid of being held up would have enjoyed visit with you immensely."

To Edsel B. Ford FDR wrote, "I am sending this note by Mr. G. Hall Roosevelt, my brother-in-law, who is familiar with the whole matter." G. Hall Roosevelt, who happened to work for General Electric as a division manager, proved himself to be an alert negotiator, but not sufficiently so to win Ford during the early stages.

However, by February 18, 1922 the American Investigation Corporation had compiled a very healthy list of subscribers, as the following partial list confirms:[1]

Name	Affiliation	Location
W.E. Boeing	President, Boeing Airplane Co.	Seattle
Edward H. Clark	President, Homestake Mining Co.	New York
Benedict Crowell	Crowell & Little Construction Co.	Cleveland

1. List dated Feb. 18, 1922 in FDR files.

Arthur V. Davis	President, Aluminum Co. of America	Pittsburgh
L.L. Dunham	Equitable Building Association	New York
Snowden A. Fahnestock	Bertron, Griscom & Co.	New York
Marshall Field, III	Capitalist	Chicago
E.M. Herr	President, Westinghouse Electric & Mfg. Co.	Pittsburgh
J.R. Lovejoy	Vice President, General Electric Company	New York
John R. McCune	President, Union National Bank	Pittsburgh
Samuel McRoberts	Capitalist	New York
R.B. Mellon	President, Mellon National Bank	Pittsburgh
W.L. Mellon	President, Gulf Oil Co.	Pittsburgh
Theodore Pratt	Standard Oil Company	New York
Franklin D. Roosevelt	Vice President, Fidelity & Deposit Co.	New York
Philip N. Wrigley	Vice President, Wm. Wrigley Co.	Chicago
Owen D. Young	Vice President, General Electric Co.	New York

The initial board of directors included National City Bank vice president Samuel McRoberts,[2] William B. Joyce, president of National Surety Company—one of FDR's competitors in the bonding and surety business—and Benedict Crowell, former Assistant Secretary of War and chairman of the board of the Cleveland construction company Crowell & Little Construction. Snowden A. Fahnestock of Bertron, Griscom was the son of New York financier Gibson Fahnestock and a partner in the stock brokerage firm of Fahnestock & Company. Gibson's brother William Fahnestock, a partner in the same firm, was director of several major corporations including Western Union and, with Allen Dulles, of Gold Dust Corporation. David Goodrich, another subscriber, was chairman of the board of B.F. Goodrich Company and a director of American Metals Company of New Mexico.

It should be noted with care that this enterprise was a private venture where the risk and the rewards were taken by experienced and clear-sighted capitalists. No criticism can be made of the financing of this venture; the criticism lies in the manner in which it acquired its main asset, the German patents.

The president's report for the year 1922, issued on January 8, 1923, summarizes the A.I.C. achievements to that date.

The German Reparations Commission refused to allow construction of large airships in Germany, and there was a delay in the completion

---

2. Samuel McRoberts figures prominently in Sutton, *Bolshevik Revolution,* op. cit.

and test of the new apparatus designed by the U.S. Bureau of Mines for the economical manufacture of helium gas, but it was considered that A.I.C. was within a few months of the time to appeal to the public for financial support. According to this report, the first stage of the work had been brought to a close by signing a contract on March 11, 1922 between the American Investigation Corporation and the Schuette-Lanz Company whereby the American Investigation Corporation secured the world patent rights on the Schuette designs and methods of construction for rigid airships. The contract provided for installment payments and included an agreement with Schuette-Lanz either to construct an airship or to provide the services of the experts to undertake construction in the U.S.

The company had "definitely determined through the Department of State that the Reparations Commission and Council of Ambassadors would not consent to the construction in Germany of the full sized ship considered by the American Investigation Corporation," and so Dr. Schuette was requested to visit the U.S. to reach a final agreement. The ultimate object, continues the report, is the establishment of the airship industry in the U.S. and "is never lost sight of; nevertheless obtaining the first ship from Germany at less cost and built by the best experts is highly desirable."

The importance of ensuring a supply of helium gas for airships was highlighted by the destruction of the British R. 38 and the Italian *Roma* airships. After consultation with the Helium Board and the chief chemist of the Bureau of Mines, a decision on the helium question was deferred until completion of the improved apparatus the Bureau was designing for the production of commercial helium. Under the terms of the agreement between the American Investigation Corporation and Washington engineer Hardesty and his associates, in addition to the $20,000 provided to cover their work before the formation of the American Investigation Corporation, certain actual out-of-pocket expenses were to be repaid for assistance in organizing the corporation. The final agreement was, however, conditional upon the signing of a contract regarding the share which Mr. Hardesty and his associates were to receive in the American Investigation Corporation and any of its subsidiary companies in return for their promotion work: above all, it required that the German patents held on behalf of the American public by the Alien Property Custodian be released to the A.I.C.

POLITICS, PATENTS, AND LANDING RIGHTS

Consequently, the A.I.C. syndicate had a major hurdle to overcome before work could begin on commercial development of airships in the

U.S. This political hurdle—to acquire the rights to the Schuette-Lanz airship construction patents—required the astute political assistance of FDR. These rights were German, but under the control of the U.S. Government. By U.S. law, seized alien property can be disposed of only by auction sale and competitive bidding. However, we find in the report of the president of A.I.C. dated May 26, 1922 that A.I.C. was then "the owner of the present Schuette-Lanz patents" and listed 24 patents and 6 patent applications originating in Germany, 6 applications originating in England, and 13 patents and 6 applications originating in the United States. The report continued: "In the U.S. 7 patents are subject to return by the Alien Property Custodian. Through filing assignments all new U.S. patents are being issued directly in care of A.I.C." How, then, did the A.I.C. syndicate obtain the German patents held in trust by the U.S.? This is particularly important because no record exists of auctions or competitive bidding. The A.I.C. report notes only:

> The interests of A.I.C. were protected by the collaboration in drawing the contracts and assignments of Mr. J. Pickens Neagle (Solicitor of the Navy Department) Franklin Roosevelt, Mr. Howe and Blackwood Brothers.

This certainly raises the question of the propriety of a U.S. Navy Department solicitor acting on behalf of a private syndicate. The German patents were sprung loose from the U.S. Government for A.I.C. by the personal intervention of Franklin D. Roosevelt. Let's see how he went about the job.

Franklin D. Roosevelt was former Assistant Secretary of the Navy, one of a series of Roosevelts to hold the job, and consequently had good political contacts in the Navy Department. In mid-1921 FDR began to probe among his old Navy friends on two questions: (1) the position of the Schuette patents and (2) the possibility of acquiring private use for the A.I.C. syndicate of the Lakehurst naval base for A.I.C. airships. On May 4, 1921 Admiral R.R. Byrd in the Office of Naval Operations acknowledged an invitation to visit FDR's estate at Campobello. Nine months later, on May 23, 1922, Commander E.S. Land, of the Navy Bureau of Aeronautics, also acknowledged an invitation to visit FDR when next in New York. Land added that there "appears to be little likelihood of my going to New York during the next three or four weeks. If you could advise me relative to the nature of your inquiries, I might be able to give you some information along the lines desired."

FDR replied to Commander Land in a letter marked *Personal,* but sent to the Navy Department, to the effect that his inquiry could not be made by telephone or letter. FDR then briefly reviewed the position of A.I.C. and stated that the company "is about to go ahead with the actual construction and operation of dirigibles," but needed to know more about the U.S. government's program for such craft: "I am not looking for any confidential information but merely such facts as I feel sure I could obtain without much difficulty were I able to go to Washington myself."

This information is, wrote FDR to Land, "for the good of the cause generally," and he then offered to defray Commander Land's expenses if he would visit New York. This apparently had little success because on June 1 FDR again requested the information and pushed even further: "Incidentally would there be any objection to our getting a copy of the Zeppelin contract? Theoretically they are all public documents."

In the final analysis, it was Pickens Neagle of the Judge Advocate Generals Office in the Navy who was the prime mover in obtaining the required German patents for A.I.C.; Neagle was obviously making himself useful to FDR in other areas, as well. On May 15, 1922 FDR wrote Neagle about Hardesty, the engineer–attorney handling the patent negotiations in Washington:

Both Mr. Fahnestock and I passed without question the very modest sum that Hardesty put in for you, [Neagle] and I feel sure that the Directors will approve of this when they meet, which will not be long now.

Navy Solicitor Neagle replied to this on June 16 to give FDR information about possible bonding business:

I am ashamed to mention so small a thing as the bond that would accompany a contract for $29,000 but things are very dull in the Government contracting line just now. The Midvale Steel and Ordnance Company just received an award of contract for 8″ gun forgings totalling a trifle under $29,000. The bond will be for an amount equal to something like 15 to 20 percent of the amount of the contract.

Again, on August 9, 1922 Neagle wrote to Louis Howe and referred to FDR's Navy papers, which were apparently undergoing the customary examination within the department before release to FDR. FDR's problem was to stop the papers "going through the hands of file clerks or inquisitive people with little sense of responsibility or meddlesome novices." The Navy Department would not release the papers without proper examination, even after Neagles' personal intervention. Writes Neagle to FDR:

I didn't see any way in which I could induce Mr. Curtis to change his view on the subject so I left it in that condition with the mental reservation however that you will be down here soon yourself and perhaps shake him loose.

The file to this point suggests that Pickens Neagle, Solicitor in the office of the Judge Advocate General of the Navy was working more on behalf of FDR than the taxpayer and the Navy Department. The contents of this file then shift to the attempt to acquire use of the German patents for A.I.C.; these letters are no longer on navy stationery, but on plain paper, without a printed address but signed by Neagle. On February 16, 1922 a letter to Howe from Neagle relates that

> our office this aft. (sic) returned to Aeronautics Bureau that suggested form of contract with endorsement saying the station might be leased to the A.I.C. and [Navy] employees furloughed for the corporation to employ.

Neagle added that, although navy officers could not direct and supervise A.I.C. employees, they could be detailed into private industry to learn the business of building airships. This private information is followed by a formal letter to Fahnestock of A.I.C. from Neagle (now wearing his official hat as Solicitor in the U.S. Navy) to confirm the fact that the navy was willing to lease the station and plant at Cape May, a permission revocable without notice. Another dated January 6, 1923 reports that Hardesty has signed a contract that "ought to be acceptable to the Corporation."

It is clear that the Schuette patents were transferred without public auction and competitive bidding, but by private agreement between the U.S. government and attorneys acting on behalf of a private company. This was a violation of the Trading with the Enemy Act.

The files also record another Navy Department employee rushing to the aid of FDR. A letter dated March 31, 1923 from M.N. McIntyre, head of the Navy News Bureau, to Louis Howe suggested that A.I.C. get hold of the "German airship being built for the Navy," as well as access to the naval base at Lakehurst. McIntyre is refreshingly open about his proposed political assistance: "If you will let me know where you stand on the Lakehurst proposition there may be something I can do to help 'grease' the ways. The same applies to the other suggestion."

We can establish from the files that FDR and his syndicate were able to call on sources of information and assistance within the Navy Department. Precisely how then did A.I.C. get control of the Schuette-Lanz patents? These were supposedly public property to be disposed of by competitive bidding. The Hardesty report of February 1921 explains the legal status of the patents and throws more light on their transfer.

The patents had been seized by the Alien Property Custodian and up to that time licensed only to the War and Navy Departments. An application was submitted January 10, 1921 by Fred Hardesty, submitting the information that a corporation (presumably A.I.C.) was to be formed that needed the patents, but Hardesty denied "that the patents themselves are of great intrinsic value." In other words, Hardesty walked a tightrope. The A.I.C. had absolute need of the patents to protect themselves from outsiders. At the same time, argues Hardesty, the patents really had no great value. They are required, he wrote to the Alien Property Custodian, "to form a moral bulwark for us against aggression of outside parties." Hardesty argued that the public interest was vitally involved and that he would be "pleased to receive information as to the value that has been set on the patents, if their value has been appraised, and as to the terms of and conditions on which they might be sold to us."

Attached to this letter in the FDR files is a "Memorandum for Mr. Hardesty" on the Johann Schuette patents that appears to have originated in the Alien Property Custodian's Office. The memorandum confirms the fact that the patents were held under the Trading with the Enemy Act of 1917, that the only right remaining to the German holder was the right to claim release, and that such claims must be settled as directed by Congress. It is unlikely, states the memorandum, that the patents would be sold by the Alien Property Custodian but, if the patents were offered for sale, "there would be little or no competition, as there are probably very few companies in existence or proposed that contemplate using them, and that therefore the prices offered would not be very high."

The memorandum then gets to the crux of the problem facing A.I.C.:

> The A.P.C. makes sales of patents, other than sales to the Government, only to American citizens at public sale to the highest bidder after public advertisement unless the President shall otherwise determine. Purchasing property from the A.P.C. for an undisclosed principal or for re-sale to a person not a citizen of the United States, or for the benefit of a person not a citizen of the United States is forbidden under severe penalty.

This leaves open the possibility that the Secretary of War or the Secretary of the Navy might recommend immediate sale to the President "as a matter of sound business policy in the public interest."

The syndicate then attempted to go the Presidential route, apparently with success. On February 4, 1921 FDR in New York wrote Hardesty in Washington, D.C., "I agree with you that we should do something immediately in regard to the Schuette patents, and at least make the try before the present administration goes out."

Then a memorandum of services rendered in the files records that on both February 9 and 17, 1921 FDR went to Washington and at least met with the Alien Property Custodian. Subsequently, Schuette granted power of attorney to Hardesty, and the patents were released by the Alien Property Custodian, although not immediately. The FDR files do not contain original signed documents on the release, only drafts of documents, but as the patents *were* ultimately released to A.I.C. it can be assumed that these working drafts are reasonably close to the final signed document. One document signed by both the Alien Property Custodian and German patentee Johann Schuette reads as follows:

> It is hereby further understood and agreed by and between the parties hereto that the price or prices at which the above enumerated patents of Johann Schuette may be sold to the American Investigation Corporation by the Alien Property Custodian are and shall be considered only a nominal value of said patents fixed and agreed on by and between the parties hereto and the actual value thereof; and that the said agent shall give, execute, and deliver to the Alien Property Custodian an unqualified release by and on the part of the said Johann Schuette and his said agent and their and each of their heirs and assigns and legal representatives of all claims, demands, etc.

It is clear from this document (1) that the Alien Property Custodian sold the patents to A.I.C., (2) that it charged A.I.C. only a "nominal price," (3) that there was no competitive bidding for the patents, and (4) that the former German holder Schuette was granted an interest either directly or indirectly. All four actions appear to be contrary to the requirements of the Trading with the Enemy Act of 1917 (see p. 000), even if there was Presidential authority for procedures (1) and (2).

Subsequently, on May 9, 1922 a contract was drawn between American Investigation Corporation and Johann Schuette. This paid Schuette $30,000 in cash, with a further $220,000 payable in monthly installments, with the last payment due not later than July 1, 1923. In the event of failure to pay by A.I.C., all rights in the patents would be turned over to Schuette. A stock allowance was granted Schuette, who in turn was to provide cooperation and technical assistance to A.I.C. There is also in the FDR files an internal memorandum that appears to be written on the typewriter normally used for FDR's letters; therefore, it is possibly a memo drawn up either by FDR or more probably by Louis Howe. This memorandum summarized the A.I.C. strategy. It lists "What we have to sell" and answers this question as follows:

1. The Schuette-Lanz patents, described as fundamental and needed by Ford's engineers also working on airship construction.

2. "A tentative contract to the Navy whereby over a million dollars in construction of a plant and building hangar are saved. This is our property as contract proposed is in exchange for license to use the Schuette patents by the Navy." In other words, A.I.C. not only was able to acquire the patents without public bidding in behind-the-

scenes political maneuvers, but also acquired the right to sell them back to the Navy. This is the kind of deal most poor taxpayers don't even dream about, although they foot the bills in the end.

3. All the data, designs, and tests of the Schuette-Lanz patents.

4. An arrangement for production of helium.

5. "A list of stockholders comprised of men of public spirit and considerable means."

6. This wasn't enough, because the next section is headed "What we Need" and lists (1) funds and (2) work. The memo then proposes an amalgamation of A.I.C. work with that of Ford engineers.

We can summarize the FDR's American Investigation Corporation deal as follows:

First, the A.I.C. was able through the personal intervention of Franklin D. Roosevelt to obtain seized patents as a gift or at a nominal price. The law required that such seized patents be offered for public bidding and not for the advantage of the former German owner. In practice, they were released behind closed doors as a result of private understanding between FDR and the Alien Property Custodian, possibly with Presidential intervention, although no trace of such assistance can be found. These patents, previously described as of no value, then became the subject of a contract involving payment of $250,000 to German citizen Schuette and the main asset of a company to promote airship construction in the U.S. On the face of the documents in the files, there is a prima facie violation of the law both by FDR and the Alien Property Custodian.

Second, these patents appear to have been released for the indirect benefit of a foreign party, a procedure subject to severe penalties under the law.

Third, the A.I.C. was able to obtain use of navy facilities valued at $1 million and official information from within the Navy Department.

Fourth, the only risk taken by the Wall Street operators was to put the enterprise together. The patents were obtained nominally, the funds came from outside New York City, and the expertise was German or that of the Ford Motor Company. Franklin Delano Roosevelt provided the political leverage to put together a deal that was on the face of it illegal and certainly a long way from the "public trust" FDR and his associates were fond of promoting in their writings and speeches.

FDR IN THE VENDING MACHINE BUSINESS

Automatic postage stamp machine sales started in 1911, but were not really efficient outlets until development of the Shermack machine in the 1920s. In 1927 the Sanitary Postage Stamp Corporation was formed to market Shermack machines for the automatic dispensing of postage stamps, previously sold in stores in loose form that exposed the user, according to the firm's sales literature, to transmission of disease. The firm's board of directors consisted of the inventor Joseph J. Shermack, Edward S. Steinam, J.A. de Camp (120 Broadway), banker George W. Naumburg, A.J. Sach, Nathan S. Smyth, and Franklin D. Roosevelt.

By April 1927 the company was selling about 450 machine installations a week. According to a letter written by FDR to A.J. Sach, vice president of the company, there were major problems with collections; in fact, ten stamp locations had not been heard from in over six months, and cash was short. FDR made the eminently sensible suggestion that salesmen should stop selling for a week and spend the released time on cash collections. Apart from such occasional suggestions, FDR's role in Sanitary Postage Stamp was nominal. Henry Morgenthau, Jr. got him into it originally and even paid the original subscription of $812.50 for FDR's initial 100 shares: "You can send me a check for the same at your leisure." FDR mailed his check the same day. The sponsors issued FDR 3000 shares of common stock "in consideration of the services you have rendered," obviously for use of his name as a bait for investors.

FDR resigned in late 1928 upon his election as Governor of New York.

FDR also was director of CAMCO (Consolidated Automatic Merchandising Corporation), but never took an active part in its flotation. CAMCO was a holding company designed to take over 70 per cent of the outstanding capital stock of a number of companies, including Sanitary Postage Stamp Corporation, and is notable because the board of directors included, not only FDR, but Saunders Norwell, who from 1926 to 1933 was president of the Remington Arms Company. In 1933 Remington Arms was sold to the Du Pont Company. In Chapter 10 we will probe the Butler Affair, an abortive attempt to install a dictatorship in the White House. Both Remington Arms and Du Pont are named in the suppressed testimony of the Congressional investigation committee. Yet in 1928 we find FDR and Saunders Norvell as codirectors in CAMCO.

GEORGIA WARM SPRINGS FOUNDATION

FDR's personal and highly commendable struggle to regain use of his legs after a 1921 polio attack led him to the mineral waters of Georgia Warm Springs. Regaining some strength, FDR decided to convert the springs, derelict and almost unused, into a business proposition to aid other polio victims.

Unfortunately, the precise source of the major funds used to develop Georgia Warm Springs cannot be determined from the FDR files as they exist today. The FDR folder on Georgia Warm Springs is relatively skimpy, and it is exceedingly unlikely that it contains all the papers relating to development of the project. The folder gives the appearance of having been screened before release to the Hyde Park archives. There is no public record of the funding for Georgia Warm Springs. Given FDR's tight personal finances during the 1920s, it is unlikely that the funds came from his personal resources. We do have some evidence for three sources of funds. First, it is more than likely that his mother, Mrs. James Roosevelt, was one. In fact, Eleanor Roosevelt wrote FDR, "Don't let yourself in for too much money and don't make Mama put in much, for if she lost she'd never get over it!"[3] Second, Edsel B. Ford is reported to have contributed funds to build the enclosure of the swimming pool, but was not a trustee of the foundation. Third, and most important, the original property was owned by corporate socialist, George Foster Peabody. According to FDR's son, Elliott Roosevelt, there was a sizeable personal note on the property itself, and this note was probably held by Peabody:

> On April 29, 1926, he acquired the derelict property, where Loyless was running ever deeper into debt. At the peak of his obligations as the new proprietor, Father had precisely $201,667.83 invested in the place in the form of a demand note, which was not completely paid off until after his death, and then only from a life insurance policy he had taken out in Warm Springs' favor. The $200,000-plus represented more than two-thirds of everything he owned. It was the only time he took such a monumental risk. Mother was terrified that if this went the way of so many of his business ventures, none of us boys could go to college, a fate which I, for one, was more than ready to face.[4]

It is significant that Elliott Roosevelt reports the existence of a $200,000 demand note that was not paid off until FDR's death. It is a reasonable supposition, moreover, that the funds were put up by some or all of the trustees. This places FDR in the same position as Woodrow Wilson, beholden to his Wall Street creditors. As these trustees were among the most powerful men in Wall Street, the charge that FDR was "in the grip of the bankers" is at least plausible.

It is therefore reasonable to suppose that the funds for Georgia Warm Springs were put up, or were under the control of, the trustees of the Georgia Warm Springs Foundation and the associated Meriweath-

3. Elliott Roosevelt, *The Untold Story*, op. cit., p. 232.
4. Ibid.

er Reserve. The trustees of the foundation in 1934 and their main business affiliations are listed below:

Georgia Warm Springs Foundation: Trustees in 1934[5]

Name of Trustee[6]	Chief Affiliations
Franklin D. Roosevelt	President of the United States of America
Basil O'Connor	Attorney, 120 Broadway, former law partner of FDR
Jeremiah Milbank	Director, Chase National Bank of N.Y.
James A. Moffett	Vice President & director, Standard Oil of New Jersey
George Foster Peabody	Original owner of the property and holder of the note on Georgia Warm Springs
Leighton McCarthy	Director of Aluminium, Ltd (Canadian subsidiary of ALCOA)
Eugene S. Wilson	Vice President, American Telephone & Telegraph (195 Broadway)
William H. Woodin	Secretary of the Treasury under FDR
Henry Pope	Director of Link-Belt Company
Cason J. Callaway	President of Callaway Mills, Inc. of New York

The trustees of Georgia Warm Springs obviously tie FDR to Wall Street. The most prominent of these were Eugene Smith Wilson (1879-1973), a vice president of American Telephone and Telegraph of 195 Broadway, New York City. Wilson also held directorships in numerous other telephone companies, including Northwestern and Southwestern Bell and the Wisconsin Telephone Company. In 1919 he was attorney for Western Electric, then became counsel for A. T. & T. before appointment as vice president in 1920. Wilson had a long association with the campaign against polio, became associated with Franklin D. Roosevelt, and in the mid-1930s was a member of the investment committee of the Georgia Warm Springs Foundation. His fellow directors on A. T. & T. included John W. Davis, who turns up in the Butler Affair (see Chapter 10).

Another of the Georgia Warm Springs trustees was James A. Moffett, a vice president of Standard Oil of New Jersey. Walter Teagle of the same company was one of the key administrators of NRA.

---

5. Taken from letter dated March 5, 1932 from Fred Botts, Business Manager at Warm Springs, to FDR at The White House.
6. Trustees also included Frank C. Root, of Greenwich, Conn., Keith Morgan of New York City, and resident trustee Arthur Carpenter.

Trustee Jeremiah Milbank was director of the Rockfeller-controlled Chase National Bank and the Equitable Trust Company.

Trustee William H. Woodin was a director of the Federal Reserve Bank of New York from 1926 to 1931 and was appointed Secretary of the Treasury by Franklin D. Roosevelt after strongly supporting FDR's 1932 election bid. Woodin resigned within six months, but because of ill health, not for any lack of interest in holding the Treasury position.

Trustee George Peabody has been identified in the previous volume[7] and was prominently associated with the 1917 Bolshevik Revolution in Russia and the Federal Reserve Bank of New York.

7. Sutton, *Bolshevik Revolution*, op. cit.

PART II

THE GENESIS
OF
CORPORATE SOCIALISM

CHAPTER 5

Making Society Work for the Few

While society is struggling toward liberty, these famous men who put themselves at its head are filled with the spirit of the seventeenth and eighteenth centuries. They think only of subjecting mankind to the philanthropic tyranny of their own social inventions.

Frederic Bastiat, The Law, *(New York: Foundation for Economic Education, 1972), p. 52*

We have described Franklin D. Roosevelt's seven-year career on "the Street" that ended with his election as Governor of New York in 1928. This description was taken from FDR's own letter files. To avoid possible misinterpretation, portions of these letters were reproduced verbatim and at length. On the basis of these letters, there is no question that FDR used political influence almost exclusively to gain bonding business while vice president of Fidelity & Deposit Co.; that significant and questionable international financial and political links surface in the case of United European Investors and International Germanic Trust; and that his intimate associates ranged from Owen D. Young, president of General Electric, a member of the élitist financial establishment, to men described by an agent of the Proudfoot Agency as a "band of crooks."

There is one persistent theme running through FDR's method of doing business: he used the political route to an extraordinary degree. In other words, FDR employed for personal gain the police power of the state as implemented by regulatory agencies, by government regulation, and by government officials through his intercession, for example, with the Alien Property Custodian, the U.S. Navy, the Federal Reserve System, and the Insurance Superintendent of the State of New York. All these political contacts made while in public service gave FDR his competitive edge in business. These are political devices, not devices born of the market place. They are devices reflecting political coercion, not voluntary exchange in the free market.

The next four chapters comprising Part Two of this book expand upon this theme of politicization of business enterprise. First, we cast a wider net to formulate the thesis of corporate socialism and identify some prominent corporate socialists, mostly associated with FDR. Then we move back in time to the 1840's to one of FDR's ancestors, Assemblyman Clinton Roosevelt of New York and his early version of NRA. This scheme is compared to Baruch's War Industries Board in 1917, the operation of the Federal Reserve System, and the Roosevelt-Hoover American Construction Council of the 1920s. Finally, in the last chapter of this part we detail the financial investment of Wall Street in the New Deal.

THE ORIGINS OF CORPORATE SOCIALISM

Old John D. Rockefeller and his 19th century fellow-capitalists were convinced of one absolute truth: that no great monetary wealth could be accumulated under the impartial rules of a competitive laissez-faire society. The only sure road to the acquisition of massive wealth was monopoly: drive out your competitors, reduce competition, eliminate laissez-faire, and above all get state protection for your industry through compliant politicians and government regulation. This last avenue yields a legal monopoly, and a legal monopoly always leads to wealth.

This robber baron schema is also, under different labels, the socialist plan. The difference between a corporate state monopoly and a socialist state monopoly is essentially only the identity of the group controlling the power structure. The essence of socialism is monopoly control by the state using hired planners and academic sponges. On the other hand, Rockefeller, Morgan, and their corporate friends aimed to acquire and control *their* monopoly and to maximize its profits through influence in the state political apparatus; this, while it still needs hired planners and academic sponges, is a discreet and far more subtle process than outright state ownership under socialism. Success for the Rockefeller gambit has depended particularly upon focusing public attention upon largely irrelevant and superficial historical creations, such as the myth of a struggle between capitalists and communists, and careful cultivation of political forces by big business. We call this phenomenon of corporate legal monopoly—market control acquired by using political influence—by the name of corporate socialism.

The most lucid and frank description of corporate socialism and its mores and objectives is to be found in a 1906 booklet by Frederick Clemson Howe, *Confessions of a Monopolist.*[1]

Frederick Howe's role in the 1917 Bolshevik Revolution and its aftermath was described in *Wall Street and the Bolshevik Revolution.*[2] Howe also emerges in Roosevelt's New Deal as consumer counsel in the Agricultural Adjustment Administration. So Howe's interest in society and its problems spans the early 20th century, from his association with Newton D. Baker, later Secretary of War, to communist Lincoln Steffens. As a special U.S. Commissioner, Howe made studies of municipal ownership of public utilities in England and in 1914 was appointed by President Wilson as U.S. Commissioner of Immigration.

What is the secret of making great wealth? Howe answers the question as follows: "Mr. Rockefeller may think he made his hundreds of millions by economy, by saving on his gas bills, but he didn't. He managed to get the people of the globe to work for him. . . ."[3]

In brief, corporate socialism is intimately related to making society work for the few.

MAKING SOCIETY WORK FOR THE FEW

This is the significant theme in Howe's book, expressed time and time again, with detailed examples of the "let others work for you" system at work. How did Mr. Rockefeller and his fellow monopolists get the globe to work for them? It went like this, according to Howe:

This is the story of something for nothing—of making the other fellow pay. This making the other fellow pay, of getting something for nothing, explains the lust for franchises, mining rights, tariff privileges, railway

1. Frederic C. Howe, *Confessions of a Monopolist* (Chicago: Public Publishing Co. 1906). The sponsor of Howe's book was the same publisher who in 1973 put out a collectivist dirge by John D. Rockefeller III entitled *The Second American Revolution.*
2. Sutton, *Bolshevik Revolution,* op. cit.
3. Howe, op. cit., p. 145.

control, tax evasions. All these things mean monopoly, and all monopoly is bottomed on legislation.

And monopoly laws are born in corruption. The commercialism of the press, or education, even of sweet charity, is part of the price we pay for the special privileges created by law. The desire of something for nothing, of making the other fellow pay, of monopoly in some form or other, is the cause of corruption. Monopoly and corruption are cause and effect. Together, they work in Congress, in our Commonwealths, in our municipalities. It is always so. It always has been so. Privilege gives birth to corruption, just as the poisonous sewer breeds disease. Equal chance, a fair field and no favors, the "square deal" are never corrupt. They do not appear in legislative halls nor in Council Chambers. For these things mean labor for labor, value for value, something for something. This is why the little business man, the retail and wholesale dealer, the jobber, and the manufacturer are not the business men whose business corrupts politics.[4]

Howe's opposite to this system of corrupt monopoly is described as "labor for labor, value for value, something for something." But these values are also the essential hall marks of a market system, that is, a purely competitive system, where market clearing prices are established by impartial interaction of supply and demand in the market place. Such an impartial system cannot, of course, be influenced or corrupted by politics. The monopoly economic system based on corruption and privilege described by Howe is a politically run economy. It is at the same time also a system of disguised forced labor, called by Ludwig von Mises the *Zwangswirtschaft* system, a system of compulsion. It is this element of compulsion that is common to all politically run economies: Hitler's New Order, Mussolini's corporate state, Kennedy's New Frontier, Johnson's Great Society, and Nixon's Creative Federalism. Compulsion was also an element in Herbert Hoover's reaction to the depression and much more obviously in Franklin D. Roosevelt's New Deal and the National Recovery Administration.

It is this element of compulsion that enables a few—those who hold and gain from the legal monopoly—to live in society at the expense of the many. Those who control or benefit from the legislative franchises and regulation and who influence the government bureaucracies at the same time are determining the rules and regulations to protect their present wealth, prey on the wealth of others, and keep out new entrants from their business. For example, to make the point clear, the Interstate Commerce Commission, created in 1880, exists to restrict competition in the transportation industry, not to get the best deal possible for shippers. Similarly, the Civil Aeronautics Board exists to protect the domestic aviation industry, not the airline traveler. For a current example, among hundreds, witness the CAB seizure in July 1974 of a

4. Howe, op. cit., pp. V-V1.

74

Philippines Air Lines (PAL) DC-10 at San Francisco airport. What sin had PAL committed? The airline merely substituted a DC-10 plane, for which equipment CAB had not granted permission, for a DC-8. Who gained? The domestic U.S. airlines, because of less competition. Who lost? The traveler denied seats and a choice of equipment. Any doubts about whose side the CAB might be on were dispelled by an article a few weeks later in *The Wall Street Journal* (August 13, 1974) entitled "CAB Is an Enthusiastic Backer of Moves to Trim Airline Service, Increase Fares." This piece contained a gem by CAB vice chairman Whitney Gillilland: "We've had too much emphasis on passenger convenience in the past." Gillilland added that the CAB must be more tolerant of capacity-packed planes, "even if it may mean somebody has to wait a day to get a flight."

In brief, regulatory agencies are devices to use the police power of the state to shield favored industries from competition, to protect their inefficiencies, and to guarantee their profits. And, of course, these devices are vehemently defended by their wards: the regulated businessmen or, as we term them, "the corporate socialists."

This system of legal compulsion is the modern expression of Frederic Bastiat's dictum that socialism is a system where everyone attempts to live at the expense of everyone else. Consequently, corporate socialism is a system where those few who hold the legal monopolies of financial and industrial control profit at the expense of all others in society.

In modern America the most significant illustration of society as a whole working for the few is the 1913 Federal Reserve Act. The Federal Reserve System is, in effect, a private banking monopoly, not answerable to Congress or the public, but with legal monopoly control over money supply without let or hindrance or even audit by the General Accounting Office.[5] It was irresponsible manipulation of money supply by this Federal Reserve System that brought about the inflation of the 1920s, the 1929 Depression, and so the presumed requirement for a Roosevelt New Deal. In the next chapter we shall examine more closely the Federal Reserve System and its originators. For the moment, let's look more closely at the arguments made by the Wall Street financier-philosophers to justify their "making society work for the few" credo.

THE CORPORATE SOCIALISTS ARGUE THEIR CASE

One can trace a literary path by which prominent financiers have pushed for national planning and control for their own benefit and that ultimately evolved into the Roosevelt New Deal.

5. A very limited audit of the Federal Reserve System was voted by Congress in 1974.

In the years following the 1906 publication of Howe's *Confessions of a Monopolist,* Wall Street financiers made book-length literary contributions, none quite as specific as Howe, but all pushing for the legal institutions that would grant the desired monopoly and the control that flows from this monopoly. From these books, we can trace New Deal ideas and the theoretical base upon which corporate socialism later came to be justified. Two themes are common in these Wall Street literary efforts. First, that individualism, individual effort, and individual initiative are out of date and that "destructive" competition, usually termed "blind competition" or "dog-eat-dog competition" is outmoded, unwanted, and destructive of human ideals. Second, we can identify a theme that follows from this attack on individualism and competition to the effect that great advantages accrue from cooperation, that cooperation advances technology, and that cooperation prevents the "wastes of competition." It is then concluded by these financier philosophers that trade associations and ultimately economic planning—in other words, enforced "cooperation"—are a prime objective for responsible and enlightened modern businessmen.

Such themes of cooperation and rejection of competition are expressed in different ways and with varying degrees of lucidity. Businessmen are not persuasive writers. Their books tend to be turgid, superficially self-seeking, and somewhat weightily pedantic. A few such examples will, however, demonstrate how Wall Street corporate socialists made their case.

Bernard Baruch was the outstanding corporate socialist whose ideas we shall examine in the next chapter. After Baruch and the Warburgs, also discussed in the next chapter, the next most prolific writer was influential banker Otto Kahn of Kuhn, Loeb & Co.

Kahn is notable for his support of both the Bolshevik Revolution and Benito Mussolini, support which he concretized in such totalitarian expressions as, "The deadliest foe of democracy is not autocracy but liberty frenzied."[6] On socialism, Otto Kahn stated his sympathy toward its objectives on many occasions. For instance, his address to the socialist League of Industrial Democracy in 1924 included the following:

> Let me point out that such measures as, for instance, the progressive income tax, collective bargaining by employees, the eight-hour day, the governmental supervision and regulation of railroads and of similar natural monopolies or semi-monopolies, are approved by the sense of justice

6. Otto H. Kahn, *Frenzied Liberty: The Myth of a Rich Man's War,* Address at University of Wisconsin, Jan. 14, 1918, p. 8.

of the business community, provided the application of such measures is kept within the limits of reason, and that they would not be repealed by business if it had the power to repeal them.

What you Radicals and we who hold opposing views differ about, is not so much the end as the means, not so much what should be brought about as how it should and can be brought about, believing as we do, that rushing after the Utopian not only is fruitless and ineffectual, but gets into the way of, and retards, progress toward realizing attainable improvement.

With all due respect, I venture to suggest that Radicalism too often tends to address itself more to theoretical perfection than to concrete amelioration; to phantom grievances, or grievances of the past, which have lost their reality, rather than to actual matters of the day; to slogans, dogmas, professions, rather than to facts.[7]

A number of these financier-philosophers from Wall Street were trustees of the Brookings Institution in Washington D.C.., responsible for many of the policy guides to achieve this desired system. Robert S. Brookings, founder of the Brookings Institution, is generally termed an economist, but Brookings himself wrote: "I certainly have no claim to that professional title. I write only as one who, through a long business experience of more than sixty years, has had much to do with manufacturing and distribution. . . ."[8] In his self-described role of businessman, Brookings published three books: *Industrial Ownership, Economic Democracy,* and *The Way Forward.* In these three books, Brookings argues that classical political economy, as reflected in the work of Adam Smith and his school,

> while *logically* convincing, was *actually* incomplete in that it made no allowance for the moral and intellectual development of man and his dependence on nationalism for its expression, so ably presented later by Adam Müller and Frederick List, or for the economic influence of mechanical production upon the relation of capital to labor.[9]

Consequently, but without presenting his evidence, Brookings rejects the free enterprise ideas of Adam Smith and accepts the statist ideas of List—also, by the way, reflected in the Hitlerian corporate state. From rejection of free enterprise Brookings finds it quite easy to deduce a "moral" system rejecting the market place and substituting an approximation to the Marxist labor theory of value. For example, Brookings writes:

> A sound system of economic morality demands therefore that instead of our paying labor merely a market wage, the minimum necessary to secure

7. Otto H. Kahn, *Of Many Things,* (New York: Boni & Liveright, 1925), p. 175.
8. R. S. Brookings, *Economic Democracy,* (New York: Macmillan, 1929), p. xvi.
9. Ibid., pp. xxi-xxii.

its services, capital should receive the market wage necessary to secure its services, and the balance should go to labor and the consuming public.[10]

From this quasi-Marxist argument Brookings constructs, rather vaguely and without detailed support, the outlines of proposals needed to combat the "evils" of the prevailing market system. Of these proposals, "The first is the revision of the anti-trust laws in such a way as to permit extensive cooperation."[11] This, argues Brookings, would have two effects: advance research and development and flatten out the business cycle. Just how these objectives follow from "cooperation" is not stated by Brookings, but he cites Herbert Hoover at length to support his argument, and particularly Hoover's article, "If Business Doesn't, Government Will."[12]

Then, like any good socialist, Brookings concludes: "Efficiently managed corporations have nothing to fear from intelligent public supervision designed to protect the public and the trade alike from grasping and intractable minorities."[13] This is necessary because, Brookings argues elsewhere, statistics indicate that most businesses operate inefficiently, "So we know from sad experience that blind or ignorant competition has failed to make its reasonable contribution through earnings to our national economic needs."[14]

In 1932 Brookings emerged from his shell in *The Way Forward* to become even more outspoken about developments in Soviet Communism:

> The verbal damning of communism now prevalently popular in the United States will get us nowhere. The decision between capitalism and communism hinges on one point. Can capitalism adjust itself to this new age? Can it move out from its old individualism, dominated by the selfish profit motive, and so create a new co-operative epoch with social planning and social control, that it can serve, better than it has, the welfare of all the people? If it can, it can survive. If it cannot, some form of communism will be forced upon our children. Be sure of that![15]

And in the same book Brookings has good words to say about another forced labor system, Italian fascism:

> Although Italy is an autocracy under the dictatorship of the Duce, every economic interest of the country is afforded opportunity for discussion and negotiation so that they may, by mutual agreement, arrive at a fair

10. R. S. Brookings, *Industrial Ownership* (New York: Macmillan, 1925), p. 28.
11. Ibid., p. 44.
12. *The Nation's Business*, June 5, 1924, pp. 7-8.
13. Brookings, *Industrial Ownership*, op. cit., p. 56.
14. Brookings, *Economic Democracy*, op. cit., p. 4
15. R. S. Brookings, *The Way Forward* (New York: Macmillan, 1932), p. 6.

compromise of their differences. The government will not permit, however, either through lockouts or strikes, any interference with the productivity of the nation, and if, in the last analysis, the groups fail to agree among themselves, the government through its minister or the labor court determines the solution of all problems. In Italy as elsewhere, however, the autocracy of capital seems to exist, and the general feeling among the working classes is that government favors the employers.[16]

What then is preeminent in Brookings' writing is his predeliction for *any* social system, communism, fascism, call it what you will, that reduces individual initiative and effort and substitutes collective experience and operation. What is left unsaid by Brookings and his fellow financier philosophers is the identity of the few running the forced labor collective. It is implicit in their arguments that the operators of the system will be the corporate socialists themselves.

From the purely theoretical proposals of Brookings we can move to those of George W. Perkins, who combined parallel proposals with some effective, but hardly moral ways of putting them into practice.

George W. Perkins was the forceful, energetic builder of the great New York Life Insurance Company. Perkins was also, along with Kahn and Brookings, an articulate expounder of the evils of competition and the great advantages to be gained from ordered cooperation in business. Perkins preached this collectivist theme as one of a series of lectures by businessmen at Columbia University in December 1907. His speech was hardly a roaring success; biographer John Garraty claims that when it was over:

> ...The President of Columbia, Nicholas Murray Butler, hurried off without a word of congratulations, evidently believing, according to Perkins, that he had unwittingly invited a dangerous radical to Morningside Heights. For Perkins had attacked some of the basic concepts of competiton and free enterprise.[17]

Garraty summarizes Perkins' business philosophy:

> The fundamental principle of life is co-operation rather than competition —such was the idea that Perkins developed in his talk. Competition is cruel, wasteful, destructive, outmoded; co-operation, inherent in any theory of a well-ordered Universe, is humane, efficient, inevitable and modern.[18]

Again, as with Brookings, we find proposals for "elimination of waste" and more "planning" for material and human resources and the concept that big business has "responsibilities to society" and is more

16. Ibid., p. 8.
17. John A. Garraty, *Right Hand Man: The Life of George W. Perkins*, (New York: Harper & Row, n.d.), p. 216.
18. Ibid.

likely to act fairly toward labor than small business. These high-sounding phrases are, of course, impressive—particularly if New York Life Insurance had lived up to its social do-good sermons. Unfortunately, when we probe further, we find evidence of wrongdoing by New York Life Insurance and investigation of this wrongdoing by the State of New York, which found a decidedly antisocial ring about New York Life's corporate behavior. In 1905-06 the Armstrong Committee (the New York State Legislature Joint Committee on Investigation of Life Insurance) found that New York Life Insurance Company had been a liberal contributor to the Republican National Committee in 1896, 1900, and 1904. Without question, these financial contributions were to advance the interests of the company in political circles. In 1905 John A. McCall, president of New York Life Insurance, was called before the New York investigating committee and proceeded to advance the idea that the defeat of Byran and free silver coinage was for him a *moral* issue. According to McCall, "... .I consented to a payment to defeat Free Silver, not to defeat the Democratic party, but to defeat the Free Silver heresy, and thank God that I did it."[19]

At the same hearing the vice president of Mutual Life Insurance also advanced the interesting concept that business had a "duty" to "scotch" unwelcome ideas and policies. The history of corporate financing of politics has hardly maintained the principles of the Constitution and a free society. More specifically, there is a gross inconsistency between the social do-good principles of cooperation advanced by Perkins and his fellow businessmen and the contemporary antisocial behavior of his own New York Life Insurance Company.

In brief, the principles of corporate socialism are but a thin veneer for the acquisition of wealth by a few at the expense of the many.

We can now look profitably at the preaching of those financiers more intimately associated with Roosevelt and the New Deal. One such financier-philosopher who expressed his collectivist ideas in writing was Edward Filene (1860-1937) The Filenes were a family of highly innovative businessmen, owners of the large department store William Filene's Sons Co. in Boston. A vice president of Filene's became one of the three musketeers running the National Recovery Administration in 1933; the other two of the triumvirate were Walter Teagle, president of Standard Oil and John Raskob, vice president of Du Pont and General Motors.

From the turn of the century Edward Filene concerned himself with

19. Quoted in Louise Overacker, *Money in Elections*, (New York: Macmillan, 1932), p. 18.

public affairs. He served as chairman of the Metropolitan Planning Commission of Boston, promotor of people's banks, and provided assistance to various cooperative movements. Filene was active in the Red Cross and the U.S. Chamber of Commerce; a founder of the League to Enforce Peace; a founder and later president of the Cooperative League, subsequently renamed the Twentieth Century Fund; and a member of the Foreign Policy Association and the Council on Foreign Relations. In Roosevelt's era Filene was chairman of the Massachusetts State Recovery Board and active in the 1936 campaign for FDR's reelection. Filene wrote several books, of which two, *The Way Out* (1924)[20] and *Successful Living in this Machine Age*, (1932),[21] express his philosophical leanings. In *The Way Out*, Filene emphasizes the theme of reducing waste, and the shortsightedness of competition and stresses the value of cooperation between business and government. Filene summarizes his argument as follows:

> Two things are clear. The first is that the business in order to be good business must itself be conducted as a public service. The second is that the finest possible public service of business men is that rendered in and through the private businesses of the world.[22]

This "public service is private business" theme is expanded in another of his books:

> My own attitude is that business must undertake social planning, but neither for the purpose of snuffing out new theories nor of preserving old ones, but because there has been a social revolution. The old order has gone and by no possibility can we bring it back. We are living in a new world. It is a world in which mass production has related everybody to everybody; and our plans, therefore, must take everybody into consideration.[23]

We also find in Filene "the road to peace is the balance of power" argument—a repeat of a 19th-century formula resurrected by Henry Kissinger in the 1970s and one that has always ultimately led to war rather than peace. Filene phrases his version as follows:

> No wonder there was war. Peace, it was soon discovered, could be maintained only by a balance of power between the larger competitors, and that balance of power was frequently upset. Eventually the whole impossible situation exploded in the greatest war of human history. The World

20. Edward A. Filene, *The Way Out*, (A Forecast of Coming Changes in American Business and Industry) (New York: Doubleday, Page, 1924).
21. Edward A. Filene, *Successful Living in this Machine Age* (New York: Simon & Schuster, 1932).
22. Filene, *The Way Out*, op. cit., p. 281.
23. Filene, *Successful Living in This Machine Age*, op. cit., p. 269.

War did not cause the world change which we have lately been noting. It was, rather, one of the phenomena of that change, just as the French Revolution was a phenomenon of the First Industrial Revolution.[24]

This theme of promotion of the public interest as a matter of primary benefit to business itself is also found in Myron C. Taylor, chairman of United States Steel Company. The public interest, Taylor argues, needs cooperation by business for rational production. The blindness of big business is clear when Taylor denies this would also be restraint of trade. Taylor omits to explain how we can adjust production to consumption without compulsion of those who may not want to cooperate. Taylor summarizes his proposals as follows:

> The point, then, is to discover what we as a nation possess and to learn to use it rather than go out in search of the new only because it is new. The primary responsibility is on industry to find ways to promote the public interest and the interests of its own producers, employees, distributors, and customers, by making and carrying out whatever constructive plans may be permissible under the present laws, acting openly and, so far as possible, in cooperation with the Government. I confess I find it extremely hard to believe that constructive, cooperative plans sincerely undertaken by a basic industry for rationally adjusting production to demand in that industry, and which avoid any attempt artificially to fix or control prices, can be fairly regarded as in restraint of trade and commerce. For the sole effect would be to remove vital impairments of production, trade, and commerce, and to promote the public interests.[25]

The Standard Oil contribution to this liturgy is expressed by Walter C. Teagle, president of Standard Oil Company of New Jersey and appointed by President Roosevelt to a top position in his NRA. Teagle phrases his version of corporate socialism as follows:

> The ills of the oil industry are peculiar to that industry and require peculiar remedies. These are modification of anti-trust laws, cooperation among producers, and the exercise of the policing power of the States.[26]

More bluntly than the others, Teagle wants the police power of the State to enforce voluntary cooperation:

> Voluntary cooperation within the industry is not sufficient to remedy its ills. It would not be sufficient even if legal restrictions on cooperation were removed, although tremendous progress would result from the removal of such restrictions.
> To protect the correlative rights of producers and to enforce adequate conservation laws the police power of the State must be employed. This is a matter for State, rather than Federal action, but cooperation among

24. Ibid., p. 79.
25. From Samuel Crowther, *A Basis for Stability*, (Boston: Little, Brown, 1932), p. 59.
26. Ibid., p. 111

various States and among the operating units of the industry will also be needed if production in the country at large is to be limited to the nation's markets. The solution of the problem therefore depends upon voluntary cooperation within the industry, upon exercise of the police power of the State, and upon cooperation among the various States concerned and among unites(sic) of the industry in the different States. To permit this both State and Federal anti-trust laws will need to be revised.[27]

These extracts reflect the basic outlook of our Wall Street financier philosophers. These were not minor figures on the Street. On the contrary, they were the powerful and influential elements and in significant cases associated with Roosevelt and the New Deal. Otto Kahn was a prime mover in the Federal Reserve System. Lamont and Perkins were key figures in the banking and insurance fields. Businessman Brookings gave his name and money to the influential research institute that produced the reports upon which much policy came to be based. Louis Kirstein, a vice president of Filene's firm, and Walter Teagle of Standard Oil became two of the three dominant men who ran the National Recovery Administration under Bernard Baruch's protégé Hugh Johnson. Bernard Baruch was probably the most prestigious Wall Streeter of all time, perhaps even exceeding in influence both Morgan and Rockefeller. We will examine Baruch and the Warburgs next.

What was the philosophy of the financiers so far described? Certainly *anything* but laissez-faire competition, which was the last system they envisaged. Socialism, communism, fascism or their variants were acceptable. The ideal for these financiers was "cooperation," forced if necessary. Individualism was out, and competition was immoral. On the other hand, cooperation was consistently advocated as moral and worthy, and nowhere is compulsion rejected as immoral. Why? Because, when the verbiage is stripped away from the high-sounding phrases, compulsory cooperation was their golden road to a legal monopoly. Under the guise of public service, social objectives, and assorted do-goodism it is fundamentally "Let society go to work for Wall Street."

27. Ibid., p. 113

CHAPTER 6

Prelude to the New Deal

Whichever party gains the day, tyrants or demagogues are most sure to take the offices.
Assemblyman Clinton Roosevelt of New York, 1841.

The full story of the construction of corporate socialism in the United States, as envisaged by the financier-philosophers identified in the previous chapter, is beyond the scope of this book, but we can gain greater perspectives through a brief look at a few facets of the historical process: for example, Clinton Roosevelt's system a century before FDR, Bernard Baruch's War Industries Board, and Paul Warburg's Federal Reserve System.

In 1841 FDR's distant cousin, Assemblyman Clinton Roosevelt of New York, proposed a scheme resembling the New Deal for economic planning and control of society by the few. Under President Woodrow Wilson in 1918 Bernard Baruch, corporate socialist *par excellence,* followed the broad outline of the Roosevelt scheme, almost certainly unknowingly and probably attributable to some unconscious parallelism of action, when he established the War Industries Board, the organizational forerunner of the 1933 National Recovery Administration. Some of the 1918 WIB corporate élite appointed by Baruch—Hugh Johnson, for example—found administrative niches in Roosevelt's

NRA. In 1922 then-Secretary of Commerce Herbert Hoover and up-and-coming Wall Streeter Franklin D. Roosevelt joined forces to promote trade associations, implementing Bernard Baruch's postwar economic planning proposals. Shortly thereafter, former socialist editor Benito Mussolini marched on Rome and established—with liberal help from the J.P. Morgan Company—the Italian corporate state whose organizational structure is distinctly reminiscent of Roosevelt's NRA. In the United States glorification of Mussolini and his Italian achievements was promoted by the ever-present financiers Thomas Lamont, Otto Kahn, and others. We will mention only briefly Wall Street involvement with both Bolshevik Russia and Hitler's Germany—both totalitarian states governed by a self-appointed élite—as full treatment of these aspects is covered in other volumes.[1].In brief, construction of FDR's National Recovery Administration was but one facet of a wider historical process—construction of economic systems where the few could profit at the expense of the many, the citizen-taxpayer-in-the-street—and all of course promoted under the guise of the public good, whether it was Stalin's Russia, Mussolini's Italy, Hitler's Germany, or Roosevelt's New Deal.

ASSEMBLYMAN CLINTON ROOSEVELT'S NRA—1841

New York Assemblyman Clinton Roosevelt was a 19th-century cousin of Franklin Delano Roosevelt and incidentally also related to President Theodore Roosevelt, John Quincy Adams, and President Martin Van Buren. Clinton Roosevelt's only literary effort is contained in a rare booklet dated 1841.[2] In essence this is a Socratic discussion between author Roosevelt and a "Producer" presumably representing the rest of us (i.e., the many). Roosevelt proposes a totalitarian government along the lines of George Orwell's 1984 society, where all individuality is submerged to a collective run by an élitist aristocratic group (i.e., the few) who enact all legislation. Roosevelt demanded ultimate, but not immediate, abandonment of the Constitution.

1. For Wall Street and the early Bolsheviks see Sutton, *Bolshevik Revolution*, op. cit. Wall Street involvement with the rise of Hitler and German Nazism is the topic of a forthcoming book.
2. Clinton Roosevelt, *The Science of Government Founded on Natural Law* (New York: Dean & Trevett, 1841). There are two known copies of this book: one in the Library of Congress, Washington D.C. and another in the Harvard University Library. The existence of the book is not recorded in the latest edition of the Library of Congress catalog, but was recorded in the earlier 1959 edition (page 75). A facsimile edition was published by Emanuel J. Josephson, as part of his *Roosevelt's Communist Manifesto* (New York: Chedney Press, 1955).

P. [Producer] But I ask again: Would you at once abandon the old doctrines of the Constitution?

A. [Author] Not by any means. Not any more than if one were in a leaky vessel he should spring overboard to save himself from drowning. It is a ship put hastily together when we left the British flag, and it was then thought an experiment of very doubtful issue.[3]

This early expression of Rooseveltian family skepticism toward the Constitution brings to mind the Supreme Court rejection in October 1934 (*Schechter Poultry Corp. v. U.S.*) of another Rooseveltian departure, an "unfettered" departure according to the court, from the rules of a constitutional society: the National Recovery Act, itself an uncanny replica of Clinton Roosevelt's 1841 program for a collective economy.

The earlier Rooseveltian system depended "First, on the art and science of cooperation. This is to bring the whole to bear for our mutual advantage."[4] It is this cooperation, i.e., the ability to bring the whole to bear for the interest of the few, that is, as we have seen, the encompassing theme of the writings and preachings of Otto Kahn, Robert Brookings, Edward Filene, Myron Taylor, and the other financier-philosophers discussed in Chapter 5. In the Roosevelt schema each man rises through specified grades in the social system and is appointed to that class of work to which he is best suited, choice of occupation being strictly circumscribed. In the words of Clinton Roosevelt:

P. Whose duty will it be to make appointments to each class?

A. The Grand Marshal's.

P. Who will be accountable that the men appointed are the best qualified?

A. A Court of physiologists, Moral Philosophers, and Farmers and Mechanics, to be chosen by the Grand Marshal and accountable to him.

P. Would you constrain a citizen to submit to their decisions in the selection of a calling?

A. No. If any one of good character insisted, he might try until he found the occupation most congenial to his tastes and feelings.[5]

Production in the system had to be equated with consumption, and the handling of "excesses and deficiencies" reflected the ideas pursued in the Swope Plan,[6] the literary base of Roosevelt's NRA. The system is certainly akin to that used in Bernard Baruch's War Industries Board during World War I. This is how Clinton Roosevelt describes the du-

3. Ibid.
4. Ibid.
5. Ibid.
6. See Appendix A.

ties of the Marshal of Creation, whose job it is to balance production and consumption:

> P. What is the duty of the Marshal of the Creating or Producing order?
> A. It is to estimate the amount of produce and manufactures necessary to produce a sufficiency in each department below him. When in operation, he shall report excesses and deficiencies to the Grand Marshal.
> P. How shall he discover such excesses and deficiencies?
> A. The various merchants will report to him the demand and supplies in every line of business, as will be seen hereafter.
> P. Under this order are agriculture, manufactures and commerce, as I perceive. What then is the duty of the Marshal of Agriculture?
> A. He should have under him four regions, or if not, foreign commerce must make good the deficiency.
> P. What four regions?
> A. The temperate, the warm, the hot region and the water region.
> P. Why divide them thus?
> A. Because the products of these different regions require different systems of cultivation, and are properly subject to different minds.[7]

Then there is a Marshal of Manufacturers overseeing the whole system—similar to Baruch's position as economic dictator in 1918 and Hugh Johnson's position as Administrator of the National Recovery Administration in 1933. The Marshal's functions are described by Clinton Roosevelt as follows:

> P. What are the duties of the Marshal of Manufacturers?
> A. He shall divide men into five general classes, according to the printed diagram.
> 1st. The manufacturers of all the means of defence against the weather.
> 2d. All kinds of viands.
> 3d. Metals and minerals.
> 4th. Chemicals.
> 5th. Machinery.
> All these have on the printed diagrams, banners, with a glory on one side and an appropriate motto on the reverse, showing the advantage each class is to all others: and by the way, we would remark, this should be universally adopted, to give a just direction to man's love of glory.
> By a reference to the chart, and what has been before observed, the duties of the officers under this department will all be obvious.

The industrial categories of 1841 are not of course precisely the categories of 1930, but a generalized similarity can be traced. The 1st division is clothing and fabrics, limited in 1841 to cotton, wool, and linen, but extended today to synthetic materials, including plastics and fibers. The 2nd division is that devoted to foodstuffs. The 3rd division is devoted to raw materials, and the 4th division includes medicines. The 5th is machinery. Today the 5th division comprises the many

---

7. Clinton Roosevelt, *The Science of Government Founded on Natural Law*, op. cit.

subdivisions of electronics, mechanical and civil engineering, but the five categories could be utilized to divide a modern economy. Clinton Roosevelt's society can be summed in his phrase, "The system should rule, and the system should look chiefly to the general good."

BERNARD BARUCH'S WARTIME DICTATORSHIP

While the Federal Reserve System and its private legal monoply of the money supply has been a fount of wealth for its operators, the ultimate goal of making society work for the few as outlined by Frederick Howe and Clinton Roosevelt can be brought about only by planned control of the whole economy, and this requires compulsory adherence of the many smaller entrepreneurs to the dictates of the few deciding the plans to be followed.

The genesis of Roosevelt's NRA, a system that included compulsory adherence by small enterpreneurs to a plan devised by big business, can be traced from Bernard Baruch's U.S. War Industries Board, established and elaborated as an emergency wartime measure. In 1915, before the U.S. entered World War I, Howard E. Coffin, then chairman of General Electric, headed the U.S. Committee on Industrial Preparedness. In company with Bernard Baruch and Daniel Willard of the Baltimore and Ohio Railroad, Coffin was also a member of the Advisory Commission to the Council of National Defense. In 1915 Bernard Baruch was invited by President Woodrow Wilson to design a plan for a defense mobilization committee. This Baruch plan subsequently became the War Industries Board, which absorbed and replaced the old General Munitions Board. Margaret L. Coit, Baruch's biographer, describes the War Industries Board as a concept similar to cooperative trade associations, a device long desired by Wall Street to control the unwanted rigors of competition in the market place:

> Committees of industry, big business and small business, both represented in Washington, and both with Washington representation back home—this could be the backbone of the whole structure.[8]

By March 1918 President Wilson acting without Congressional authority, had endowed Baruch with more power than any other individual had been granted in the history of the United States. The War Industries Board, with Baruch as its chairman, became responsible for building all factories and for the supply of all raw material, all products, and all transportation, and all its final decisions rested with chair-

8. Margaret L. Coit, *Mr. Baruch* (Boston: Houghton, Mifflin, 1957), p. 147.

man Bernard Baruch. In brief, Baruch became economic dictator of the United States, or "Marshal of Manufacturers" in Clinton Roosevelt's scheme. Yet, as Margaret Coit points out, ". . . the creation of this office was never specifically authorized by an Act of Congress."[9]

So by the summer of 1918 Baruch, with extraordinary and unconstitutional powers, had, in his own words, "finally developed a scheme of positive 'control' over the major portion of the industrial fabric . . . Success bred courage for more success, and trade after trade was taken under control with an increasing willingness on the part of the interests affected."[10]

At the time of the Armistice the W.I.B. comprised Baruch (chairman), Alexander Legge of International Harvester (vice chairman), with E.B. Parker and R.S. Brookings (whose ideas we have already examined) in charge of price fixing. Assistants to the chairman were: Herbert Bayard Swope, brother of Gerard Swope of General Electric; Clarence Dillon of the Wall Street firm Dillon, Read & Co.; Harrison Williams; and Harold T. Clark.[11]

Baruch's final report on W.I.B. activity was much more than a history of its operations; it was also a specific plan and recommendation for economic planning in peacetime. Baruch was not content merely to summarize the lessons to be learned for planning in war or for industrial preparedness in time of uneasy peace. On the contrary, Baruch's conclusions were directed, in his own words, to the "industrial practices of peace" and to make recommendations "relating to the business practices of normal times." The bulk of the conclusions relate to change-over of a *planned* wartime economic system to a *planned* peacetime economic system, and even the suggestions for wartime practice are related to peacetime functions. Baruch suggested that the most important "direct war lessons to be derived" from the operation of the War Industries Board were:

9. Ibid., p. 172.
10. Bernard M. Baruch, *American Industry in the War: A Report of the War Industries Board* (March 1921), with an introduction by Hugh S. Johnson (New York: Prentice-Hall, 1941) (including "a reprint of the report of the War Industries Board of World War I, Mr. Baruch's own program for total mobilization of the nation as presented to the War Policies Commission in 1931, and current material on priorities and price fixing").
11. For a complete list of W.I.B. personnel see Grosvenor B. Clarkson, *Industrial America in the World War* (New York: Houghton, Mifflin, 1923), Appendix III. In the light of Chapter 11, below, it is intriguing to note numerous W.I.B. committee members with offices at 120 Broadway including Murry W. Guggenheim, Stephen Birch (Kennecott Copper), Edward W. Brush (American Smelting and Refining), F. Y. Robertson (United States Metals Refining Co.), Harry F. Sinclair (Sinclair Refining Co.), Charles W. Baker, (American Zinc), and Sidney J. Jennings (United States Smelting, Refining and Mining Co.)

1. The establishment of a peacetime skeleton organization with 50 commodity divisions, meeting to keep abrest of the development of industry and develop information. The thrust of this proposal was that the information needed for peacetime planning should be collected and that the direction of the organization should stem from large-scale or major industry.
2. That the government "should devise some system for protecting and stimulating internal production of certain raw materials used in war," and
3. That war-related industries should be encouraged by the government to maintain skeleton organizations for wartime use.

Apart from these quite elementary suggestions, Baruch is exclusively concerned in the report with peacetime "planning." First we are presented with the canard that, in some unstated way, "the processes of trade" have changed and are now forced to give way before "certain new principles of supervision." This non sequitur is followed by the statement:

> We have been gradually compelled to drift away from the old doctrine of Anglo-American law, that the sphere of Government should be limited to preventing breach of contract, fraud, physical injury and injury to property, and that the Government should exercise protection only over non-competent persons.

It is necessary, writes Baruch, for government "to reach out its arm" to protect "competent individuals against the discriminating practices of mass industrial power." While Baruch points to Federal control of the railroads and the merchant fleet, he does not state *why* the representatives of big business would be the best fitted to exercise this control. In other words, why the fox is proposed as the most competent being to run the chicken coop is left unstated. Baruch then slashes at the Sherman and Clayton anti-trust laws on the grounds that these statutes are merely efforts to force industry into the mold of "simpler principles sufficient for the conditions of a bygone day," and lauds the achievement of the War Industries Board because it had constructed hundreds of trade associations controlling prices and methods of distribution and production:

> Many businessmen have experienced during the war, for the first time in their careers, the tremendous advantages, both to themselves and to the general public, of combination, of cooperation and common action with their natural competitors.

If these cooperative attributes are not continued, argues Baruch, then businessmen will be tempted "and many of them will be unable to resist" to conduct "their business for private gain with little reference to general public welfare." On the other hand, trade associations can be of the greatest public benefit to achieve the desired end of cooperation. Baruch concludes:

> The question, then is what kind of Government organization can be devised to safeguard the public interest while these associations are preserved to carry on the good work of which they are capable.

Baruch, like any good socialist, proposes government organizations to develop these principles of cooperation and coordination.

If the reader will shed for a moment the idea of a mutual antagonism between communism and capitalism, he will readily see in the writing of Bernard Baruch the basic objectives of Karl Marx writing in *The Communist Manifesto*. What is different between the two systems are the names of the élitist few running the operation known as state planning; the vanguard of the proletariat in Karl Marx is replaced by the vanguard of big business in Bernard Baruch.

Who would gain from Baruch's proposal? The consumer? Not at all, because consumer interests are *always* protected by free competition in the market place, where goods and services are produced at the least cost, in the most efficient manner, and the consumer is given maximum choice among competing producers. The gainers from Baruch's proposals would be the few who control major industrial sectors—particularly iron and steel, raw materials, electrical goods, that is, those industries already well established and fearful of competition from more enterprising newcomers. In other words, the gainers from his proposal would be Bernard Baruch and the Wall Street coterie that effectively controls big business through its interlocking directorships. The gut issue then is: who benefits from these proposals for trade associations and government coordination of industry? The principal, indeed the only major benefactors—apart from the swarms of academic advisers, bureaucrats, and planners—would be the financial élite in Wall Street.

So here we have, in Baruch's own words and ideas, an implementation of Frederic Howe's injunction to "make society work for you," the monopolist. This is also in the form of a proposal comparable to Clinton Roosevelt's system. There is no evidence that Baruch had heard of Clinton Roosevelt. There was no need for him to have done so; the advantages of restraint of trade and opportunity have always been obvious to the already established enterprise. It will therefore come as no surprise to find Bernard Baruch at the very core of the Roosevelt NRA, which itself parallels many of Baruch's post-war proposals, and who had a $200,000 investment in the election of FDR. It explains why Baruch's World War I personnel turn up in the New Deal. General

91

Hugh Johnson, for example, spent the 1920s studying industrial organization at Baruch's expense and emerged in 1933 as boss of the National Recovery Administration. It also explains why Franklin Delano Roosevelt, a Wall Streeter himself for much of the 1920s, was cofounder with Herbert Hoover—another Wall Streeter in the 1920s—of the first of the trade associations proposed by Baruch, the American Steel Construction Association, discussed in the next chapter.

Parallel to Bernard Baruch's ideas, which came to fruition in the NRA, there is a much more successful contemporary example of corporate socialism in practice: the Federal Reserve System.

PAUL WARBURG AND CREATION
OF THE FEDERAL RESERVE SYSTEM

Although many had a hand, or thought they had, in fashioning the Federal Reserve legislation, essentially the system was the brain child of one man: Paul Warburg, brother of Max Warburg, whom we met in Chapter 3. Paul Moritz Warburg (1868-1932) descended from the German banking family of Oppenheim. After early training in the offices of Samuel Montagu & Co. in London and the Banque Russe Pour le Commerce Étranger in Paris, Warburg entered the family banking house of M.M. Warburg & Co. in Hamburg. In 1902 Warburg became a partner in the New York banking house of Kuhn, Loeb & Co. while continuing as a partner in Warburg's of Hamburg. Five years later, in the wake of the financial panic of 1907, Warburg wrote two pamphlets on the U.S. banking system: *Defects and Needs of our Banking System* and *A Plan for a Modified Central Bank*.[12]

In the years after 1907, Warburg lost no opportunity to speak and write publicly about the need for banking and currency reform in the United States, and in 1910 he formally proposed a United Reserve Bank of the United States. This plan developed into the Federal Reserve System, and Warburg was appointed by President Woodrow Wilson a member of the first Federal Reserve Board. Major criticism of Warburg erupted during World War I because of brother Max's role in Germany, and he was not reappointed to the Board in 1918. However, from 1921 to 1926, after criticism had abated, Warburg became a member of the Advisory Council of the Federal Reserve Board and served as its president from 1924 to 1926.

After passage of the 1913 Federal Reserve Act, Warburg and his

12. See also Paul Warburg, *The Federal Reserve System, Its Origin & Growth; Reflections & Recollections* (New York: Macmillan, 1930)

banking associates promptly set about using the legal banking monopoly for their own ends and purposes, as suggested by Frederic Howe. In 1919 Warburg organized the American Acceptance Council and served as chairman of its executive committee in 1919-20 and as its president in 1921-22. Then in 1921 Warburg organized and became chairman of the private International Acceptance Bank, Inc. while still serving on the Advisory Council of the Federal Reserve Board. In 1925 Warburg added two more private acceptance banks: the American and Continental Corp. and the International Acceptance Trust Co. These banks were affiliated with the Warburg-controlled Bank of the Manhattan Company. As an aside it may be noted that Paul Warburg was also a director of the American IG Chemical Corp., the American subsidiary of IG Farben in Germany. IG Farben was prominent in bringing Hitler to power in 1933 and manufactured the Zyklon-B gas used in Nazi concentration camps. Warburg was a founding member of the Carl Schurz Memorial Foundation, a propaganda organization established in 1930, a director of the prestigious Council on Foreign Relations, Inc., and a trustee of the Brookings Institution.

But it was through a virtual monopoly of U.S. acceptance banking, achieved by the International Acceptance Bank Inc. and its affiliated units, that Warburg was able to get society to go to work for the Warburgs and their banking friends. Revisionist historian Murray Rothbard has examined the origins of the 1920s inflation that led to the collapse of 1929 and makes this pertinent observation:

> While purchase of U.S. securities has received more publicity, bills bought were at least as important and indeed more important than discounts. Bills bought led the inflationary parade of Reserve credit in 1921 and 1922, were considerably more important than securities in the 1924 inflationary spurt, and equally important in the 1927 spurt. Furthermore, bills bought alone continued the inflationary stimulus in the fatal last half of 1928.[13]

What were these "bills bought" pinpointed by Rothbard as the key culprit of the 1929 depression? Bills bought were acceptances, and almost all were bankers acceptances.

Who created the acceptance market in the United States, largely unknown before 1920? Paul Warburg.

Who gained the lions' share of this acceptance business at artificially low subsidized rates? The International Acceptance Bank, Inc.

Who was the International Acceptance Bank, Inc? Its chairman was Paul Warburg, with Felix Warburg and James Paul Warburg as codi-

13. Murray N. Rothbard, *America's Great Depression* (Los Angeles: Nash Publishing Corp. 1972), p. 117.

rectors. However, a closer look at the make-up of the banks (see below page 95) suggests that it was a vehicle representing the financial élite of Wall Street.

Did the Warburgs and their Wall Street friends know where their financial policy would lead? In other words, did their financial policies of the 1920s have elements of deliberation? There exists a memorandum by Paul Warburg that clearly notes that banks had the capability to prevent inflation:

> If the Government and the banks of the United States were helpless automatons, inflation, no doubt, would have to ensue. But it is insulting our banks to have the impression go out that they should not be capable of cooperating in some common plan of protection such, for instance, as keeping all cash reserves higher than required by the law, if indeed such a step should become advisable for the greater safety of the country.[14]

Consequently, Rothbard quite rightly concludes:

> Surely, Warburg's leading role in the Federal Reserve System was not unconnected with his reaping the lion's share of benefits from its acceptance policy.[15]

In brief, the policy of creating acceptances at subsidized artificial rates was not only inflationary, but was the most important factor, apparently a deliberate banking policy, leading to the inflation of the 1920s and the ultimate collapse in 1929, thus making FDR's New Deal or national economic planning appear necessary. Further, this was, as Rothbard states, ". . . the grant of special privilege to a small group at the expense of the general public." In other words, Wall Street made American society go to work for a financial oligopoly.

Warburg's revolutionary plan to get American society to go to work for Wall Street was astonishingly simple. Even today, in 1975, academic theoreticians cover their blackboards with meaningless equations, and the general public struggles in bewildered confusion with inflation and the coming credit collapse, while the quite simple explanation of the problem goes undiscussed and almost entirely uncomprehended. The Federal Reserve System is a legal private monopoly of the money supply operated for the benefit of a few under the guise of protecting and promoting the public interest.

Revolutionary? Yes indeed! But as one of Warburg's admiring biographers commented:

> Paul M. Warburg is probably the mildest-mannered man that ever personally conducted a revolution. It was a bloodless revolution: he did not

14. United States Senate, Hearings, *Munitions Industry*, Part 25, op. cit., p. 8103.
15. Murray Rothbard, *America's Great Depression*, op. cit., p. 119.

attempt to rouse the populace to arms. He stepped forth armed simply with an idea. And he conquered. That is the amazing thing. A shy, sensitive man, he imposed his idea on a nation of a hundred million people.[16]

How did this revolution of Warburg's differ from socialist revolution? Only in the fact that under socialism, once the revolution is achieved and the power of the state gathered into the right ideological hands, the accrued personal rewards are not usually as substantial— although the fiefdoms carved out by national socialist Hitler and the modern Soviets may challenge this observation—nor are the results so veiled. The monetary dictatorship of the Soviets is obvious. The monetary dictatorship of the Federal Reserve System is muted and evaded.

We should then take a closer look at the International Acceptance Bank, the vehicle used for this revolutionary exploitive maneuver because it provides valid signals that Wall Street would also have a real interest in national economic planning and an FDR type of New Deal.

THE INTERNATIONAL ACCEPTANCE BANK, INC.

The bank was founded in 1921 in New York and affiliated with Warburg's Bank of the Manhattan Company. However, the board of directors suggests that the most important elements in Wall Street also had a significant interest and control in and profited from the International Acceptance Bank. Further, we find a striking link-up between its affiliated financial institutions and a general scheme to establish corporate socialism in the United States.

As we have noted, Paul M. Warburg was chairman of the board: his brother Felix, also a partner in Kuhn Loeb & Co., and his son James P. Warburg were codirectors. The vice chairman of the board was John Stewart Baker, also president and director of the Bank of Manhattan Trust Co. and International Manhattan Co., as well as chairman of the executive committee and director of the Manhattan Trust Co. Baker was also director of the American Trust Co. and the New York Title and Mortgage Co.

F. Abbot Goodhue was president and director of International Acceptance Bank, on the board of the other Warburg banks, and a director of the First National Bank of Boston. Other directors of the International Acceptance Bank were Newcomb Carlton, director of the Rockefeller-controlled Chase National Bank, the Morgan-controlled Metropolitan Life Insurance Co., and other such major companies as

16. Harold Kellock, "Warburg, the Revolutionist," in *The Century Magazine*, May 1915, p. 79.

the American Express Co., the American Sugar Refining Co., and the American Telegraph and Cable Co. Newcomb Carlton was also a director of American Telegraph and Cable and a director of American International Corporation, a company intimately involved with the Bolshevik Revolution.[17] Another director of International Acceptance Bank who was also a director of American International Corp. was Charles A. Stone, located at 120 Broadway and a director of the Federal Reserve Bank from 1919 to 1932. Bronson Winthrop was also a director of both American International Corp. and International Acceptance Corp. Thus, three directors of International Acceptance Bank had interlocking directorships with American International Corp., the key vehicle in U.S. involvement in the Bolshevik revolution.

Another director of International Acceptance Bank was David Franklin Houston, who was also a director of the Carnegie Corp., the Morgan-controlled Guaranty Trust Co., U.S. Steel, and A.T.& T., as well as president of the Mutual Life Insurance Co. Other directors of I.A.B. included Philip Stockton, president of the First National Bank of Boston, and a director of A.T. & T., General Electric, International Power Securities, and many other companies; William Skinner, director of Irving Trust Co., Equitable Life Assurance, and the Union Square Savings Bank; Charles Bronson Seger, director of Aviation Corp., Guaranty Trust Co., and W.A. Harriman; Otto V. Schrenk, director of Agfa Ansco Corp., Krupp Nirosta, and Mercedes Benz Co.; and Henry Tatnall, director of the Girard Trust Co. Paul Warburg was also a director of Agfa Ansco, Inc., a firm 60 per cent owned by I.G. Farben and a "front" for I.G. in the United States.

In sum, the directors of International Acceptance Bank reflected the most powerful sectors of Wall Street: the Morgans, the Rockefellers, and Harriman, as well as the Boston bankers.

Further, there was a lifelong and intimate Warburg association with the Roosevelts from childhood to the New Deal. This Warburg–Roosevelt association is illustrated by an extract from James P. Warburg's memoirs: "It so happened that I had known the President-elect's eldest son, James Roosevelt, for some years, because he had been living in one of the cottages on my Uncle Felix's estate in White Plains."[18]

Later the same James P. Warburg became adviser to President Franklin D. Roosevelt on domestic and international monetary affairs. The Warburg's deep interest in the NRA program is reflected in a 1933 Warburg memorandum to FDR:

17. See Sutton, *Bolshevik Revolution*, op. cit., Chapter 8.
18. James P. Warburg, *The Long Road Home: The Autobiography of a Maverick* (Garden City: Doubleday, 1964), p. 106.

Memorandum for the President: Domestic Currency Problem. The Administration has, in my judgment, never faced a more serious situation than it does today. The entire recovery program, which is the heart of its policy, is jeopardized by uncertainty and doubt in the monetary field. The National Recovery Act cannot possibly function to any useful end if there is fear of currency depreciation of an unknown amount and fear as to monetary experimentation. There has already been a tremendous flight of capital, and this flight will continue at an increasing pace so long as uncertainty prevails.[19]

Then, following the Warburg proclivity for monopoly, James Warburg recommended to FDR that *all* monetary ideas, actions, and decisions be centralized in the Treasury Department and the Federal Reserve Board.

Obviously, this proposal would ensure that all monetary decisions were made by the élitist group associated with the International Acceptance Bank and the Federal Reserve System. The Secretary of the Treasury in July 1933, when James Warburg wrote his memorandum to FDR, was William H. Woodin, who had been director of FRB of New York from 1925 to 1931. We can also cite FDR's own associations with the Federal Reserve System. His "favorite uncle" Frederic Delano was appointed vice chairman of the Federal Reserve Board by President Woodrow Wilson in 1914, and from 1931 to 1936 Delano served as chairman of the board of the Federal Reserve Bank of Richmond, Virginia. FDR appointed Delano chairman of the National Resources Planning Board in 1934.

In 1933-34 the United States faced the greatest financial crisis in its history. And what did FDR do? He called in as the financial doctors the very operators responsible for the crisis—as sensible a policy as allowing the lunatics to run the asylum.

So we find associations between Franklin D. Roosevelt, the Warburg family, and the Warburg-inspired central banking system ranging from childhood to Warburg's appointment as a key monetary adviser to FDR. We shall see later that it was Warburg who determined the final shape of the National Industrial Recovery Administration. On the other hand, the Warburg family and their Wall Street friends controlled the private monopoly money supply known as the Federal Reserve System and through the International Acceptance Bank exploited that monopoly for their own purposes.

The Founding Fathers demonstrated a profound wisdom and insight into the dangers of a monopoly of paper money issue that is reflected in Article I, Section 9 of the U.S. Constitution: "No State shall

19. *Franklin D. Roosevelt and Foreign Affairs*, Vol. I, p. 325. Memorandum of James P. Warburg to Roosevelt, July 24, 1933.

. . . make any Thing but gold and silver Coin a Tender in Payment of Debts. . . ."

A constitutional challenge to the issue of Federal Reserve notes by a private banking monopoly, the Federal Reserve System, is overdue. Hopefully, the value of the dollar will not have to be reduced to zero, as the mark was in post-World War I Germany, before such a challenge is initiated and sustained by the Supreme Court of the United States.

CHAPTER 7

Roosevelt, Hoover,
and the Trade Councils

People of the same trade seldom meet together even for merriment and
diversion, but the conversation ends in a conspiracy against the public,
or on some contrivance to raise prices.
  Adam Smith, An Inquiry into the Nature and Causes of the Wealth of
Nations *(London: George Routledge, 1942), p. 102.*

The idea of getting society to work for a privileged group within that
society originated neither among the corporate socialists in Wall Street,
nor in the financial community at large, nor even among the Marxian
socialists. In fact, the notion predates our own industrial society, and
there is an interesting parallel between the codes of New Deal America
(which we shall examine later) and 13th-century trade legislation in
England.[1]

A MEDIEVAL NEW DEAL

In 1291 the tanners of Norwich, England were brought before the local
court charged with organizing and coding their tanning activities to

1. See Erwin F. Meyer, "English Medieval Industrial Codes" in *The American Federa-
   tionist,* January 1934. Meyer draws some fascinating parallels between the medieval
   guilds and NRA practice under Roosevelt. In medieval times the result, as in the
   1930s was to create "an oligarchy of capitalists" in the English economy.

the detriment of local citizens. Two years later in 1293, the cobblers and saddlemakers of Norwich were faced with similar charges. By "greasing" the legislators, the political power structure of medieval Norwich was brought around to the view that perhaps the tanners needed protection, after all. This protection came to incorporate the same basic principles of economic planning that almost 700 years later were put forward in the Roosevelt New Deal. So in 1307 the tanning industry of Norwich was legally coded and wages and conditions of work prescribed, all done under the guise of protecting the consumer, but in practice granting a legal monopoly to the tanners.

In the decade before the New Deal, during the 1920s Wall Streeter Roosevelt was active on behalf of business to promote these same basic ideas of using the police power of the state to restrain trade, to advance cooperation, and to utilize government regulation to inhibit unwelcome competition from more efficient outsiders. The trade associations of the 1920s were more demure in their proposals than the 13th-century Norwich tanners, but the underlying principle was the same.

Unfortunately, Franklin D. Roosevelt's role in the Wall Street of the 1920s has been ignored by historians. Daniel Fusfield does correctly observe that FDR "took an active part in the trade association movement that was to develop into the N.R.A. of the early New Deal;"[2] on the other hand Fusfield, who offers the only extensive description of FDR's business activities, concludes that his attitude toward business was "a curious mixture." FDR, says Fusfield, was "insistent that mere profits were not a full justification for business activity," that a businessman must also "have the motive of public service." This to Fusfield was inconsistent with participation "in a number of outright speculative and promotional ventures that had little to do with serving the public."[3]

Fusfield and his fellow historians of the Roosevelt era have failed to note that "public service" for a businessman is absolutely consistent with "profit maximization;" in fact, public service is the easiest and certainly the most lucrative road to profit maximization. Further, the riskier and more speculative the business, presumably the greater is the advantage to be gained from public service.

When we take this more realistic view of social do-goodism, then Wall Streeter Roosevelt's attitude toward business is not at all "curious." It is in fact a consistent program of profit maximization.

2. Daniel R. Fusfield, *The Economic Thought of Franklin D. Roosevelt and the Origins of the New Deal*
3. *Ibid.*

THE AMERICAN CONSTRUCTION COUNCIL

The American Construction Council (A.C.C.), formed in May 1922, was the first of numerous trade associations created in the 1920s, devices used to raise prices and reduce output. The original proposal and the drive for the council came from Secretary of Commerce Herbert Hoover, and the council operated under the leadership of Franklin D. Roosevelt, then just beginning his Wall Street career following his service as Assistant Secretary of the Navy. The stated public objectives of the A.C.C. were a "code of ethics" (a euphemism for restraint of trade), efficiency, and standardization of production. Most importantly, but less publicized, the A.C.C. was to provide the industry with an opportunity to fix its own price and production levels without fear of antitrust prosecutions by the government. *The New York Times* reported:

> It is these tremendous possibilities, in dedication to the public service and the elimination of waste, that have fired the imaginations of Mr. Hoover and Mr. Roosevelt and invited them to accept positions of leadership in the movement.[4]

Like the price-fixing committees of Baruch's War Industries Board, the A.C.C. was in effect a primitive industry association, although the high-sounding stated object of the council was:

> . . .to place the construction industry on a high plane of integrity and efficiency and to correlate the efforts toward betterment made by existing agencies through an association dedicated to the improvement of the service within the construction industry. . . ."[5]

and so to stabilize conditions for the benefit of the industry, labor, and the general public. This objective was also Baruch's objective for peacetime trade associations: to regulate industry under government control, while citing the public good. In the American Construction Council the public good was announced as the elimination of the scandals found by the Lockwood Commission investigating the New York building industry. However, as that scandal dealt in great part with exclusive dealing and similar coercive conditions forced upon contractors and erectors by the United States Steel Corporation and Bethlehem Steel, the announced public good makes little sense. These industry giants were controlled by the Morgan interests on Wall Street

---

4. *The New York Times,* May 15, 1922, p. 19.
5. Cited in Fusfield, *Economic Thought,* op. cit., p. 102.

who were, as we shall see, also at the root of the A.C.C. proposal. In brief, the alleged antisocial conditions to be solved by a trade association could have been halted much more simply and effectively by a memorandum from J.P. Morgan and his associates; there was no necessity to promote a trade association to halt such abuses. So we must look elsewhere for the reason for trade associations. The real reason, of course, is to protect industry from unwelcome competition and to establish monopoly conditions for those already in the business. As Howe told us, a legal monopoly is the sure road to profit. It was formation of this legal monopoly that induced Roosevelt and Herbert Hoover to join hands against the public interest, although, according to Freidel:

> FDR's friend Elliott Brown, warned him against the "socialistic" tendencies of these associations and of Hoover specifically. Socialistic, because the moment a combination is formed, the Government will assert an interest and will express that interest through the medium of some clerk in the Department of Commerce, who will approve or disapprove many matters affecting the initiative and welfare of all peepul (sic).[6]

FDR's role is not really surprising. He was then attempting to get a business career underway. He had political contacts and was more than willing, indeed eager, to use these. On the other hand, there is an odd dichotomy in the ideas and practices of Herbert Hoover in this area of the relationship between government and business. Herbert Hoover declared his adherence to the principles of free enterprise and individual initiative and his suspicion of government intervention. These assertions were mixed with other contrary statements encouraging, indeed authorizing, government intervention on almost trivial grounds. Unfortunately, Herbert Hoover's *Memoirs,* the only finally authoritative source, do not resolve these conflicts. The American Construction Council is not mentioned in Hoover's *Memoirs,* although Volume II, "The Cabinet and the Presidency," underlines the evils of government intervention in the economy, pointing to communism, socialism, and fascism to comment, "This left wing cure for all business evil" now appears as "national planning." Hoover added that business "abuses" were only "marginal" and rather than have government intervention" . . . beyond and better than even that was cooperation in the business community to cure its own abuses."[7]

On the other hand, Hoover's private correspondence with Roosevelt on the American Construction Council suggests that Hoover, while in favor of government intervention, was careful to disguise this continu-

6. Freidel, *The Ordeal,* op. cit., p. 152.
7. *The Memoirs of Herbert Hoover:* The Cabinet and the Presidency 1920-1933, (London: Hollis and Carter 1952), p. 67.

ing interest for fear of bringing public opposition down upon his own head and ruining the proposal. A letter from Hoover to Roosevelt dated June 12, 1923 makes this point:

June 12, 1923

Franklin D. Roosevelt, Vice Pres.
Fidelity and Deposit Company of Maryland
120 Broadway
New York City
My Dear Roosevelt:
    I am in somewhat of a quandary about your telegram of June 7th. I had hoped that the Construction Council would be solely originated from the industries without pressure from the Administration. Otherwise it will soon take on the same opposition that all Governmental touches to this problem immediately accrue.
    The vast sentiment of the business community against Government interference tends to destroy even a voluntary effort if it is thought to be carried on at Government inspiration.
Yours faithfully
Herbert Hoover

In any event, the American Construction Council was a cooperative association of business, labor, and government

formed at Washington on June 19 at the suggestion and under the guidance of Secretary Hoover of the Department of Commerce (who) has taken the first steps toward putting into operation a program of construction effort which, it is hoped, will eliminate many of the evils which have developed in the industry during the past decade.[8]

Thus, it was free enterpriser Herbert Hoover who became the sponsor of the first of the trade associations, the American Construction Council, which was designed to include

architects, engineers, construction labor, general contractors, sub-contractors, materials and equipment manufacturers, material and equipment dealers, bond, insurance and real estate interests and the construction departments of Federal, State and municipal governments.[9]

The organization meeting of the American Construction Council was held at FDR's house in New York and attended by about 20 persons. This group discussed the concept of the council and particularly whether it

should be a clearing house for the different national associations, a clerical clearing house, or whether it should be an active, agressive (sic) militant organization in this service of the public good of the construction industry.[10]

8. *The New York Times,* July 9, 1922, VIII 1:3.
9. *The New York Times,* May 15, 1922, p. 19, col. 8.
10. Minutes of the Executive Board of the American Construction Council, June 20, 1922. FDR Files, Group 14: American Construction Council.

It was unanimously decided that the council should be a militant aggressive organization and not just a clearing house for information. This concept was discussed with Dwight Morrow of the J.P. Morgan firm; with Mr. Dick, secretary to Judge Gary of the U.S. Steel Corporation; with Gano Dunn, president of J.G. White Engineering Corporation; and with Stone & Webster. It is interesting to note that most of these persons and firms are prominent in my previous volume, *Wall Street and the Bolshevik Revolution.*

After the financial establishment had expressed support of A.C.C., the construction industry at large was approached for its reaction. This preliminary work culminated in an organizational meeting at the Hotel Washington, Washington D.C., on Tuesday, June 20, 1922. Franklin D. Roosevelt was elected president of the council, and John B. Larner, vice president of the American Bankers Association, was elected treasurer. The chairman of the finance committee was Willis H. Booth of Guaranty Trust Company. The committee then established its committees and laid down priorities for its problems.

Roosevelt's interpretation of the causes for the problems of the construction industry were reported by *The New York Times*: "Muddling through has been the characteristic method employed by the construction industry for the last few years. There has been no system, no cooperation, no intensive national planning."

After pointing out that a railroad man is not laid off because of bad weather, Roosevelt commented:

> In construction work, however, we have that great bugbear in our economic life, the seasonal job. All the work is crowded into the summer months, none of the work is carried on during the winter. The results of this piling on are plain. In the summer we have scarcity of labor and skyrocketing of prices, in the winter unemployment and cutting of incomes. The only thing that lasts throughout the year is the bitterness of men engaged in the work.[11]

How did FDR propose to change all this?

> A large part of the work can be spread over the year. There is no reason in the world why a skilled mechanic living in New York, for instance, should be called down in June to help put up a public building in Georgia. Georgia can build in seasons of the year in which it is impossible for New York to build; so can Louisiana, so can all the Southern States.

---

11. *The New York Times*, June 4, 1922. One searches in vain for a practicable, workable proposal to solve the alleged problems of the construction industry. The most valid suggestions put forward by Roosevelt and his fellow planners required changing the weather to allow year-round construction or movement of men and materials by "planning." Of course, a market system moves men and materials automatically, a point presumably unknown to FDR.

Roosevelt's suggestion, an aimless non sequitur, was that the construction industry must "get together on this situation: move construction materials during off season and spread labor around." At an early board of governors' meeting, held at FDR's home in New York on May 16, 1923, FDR called attention to the road the council had followed: "The American Construction Council was organized, but frankly, it has not done one darned thing from that time to this except collect dues from some 115 different organizations, I think."

FDR put the basic choice to the assembled governors: did they want to continue the old way, "Build all we can, paying any old price as long as we get the orders?" Because if that was the case, said FDR, "We might just as well adjourn." On the other hand, he continued, that did not appear to be the view of the majority, and "We want to go back to the real basic purpose of the Council, which was to prevent this sort of thing." Then followed a series of proposed resolutions, adopted unanimously, that would have the effect of slowing down construction. The council continued to have its problems, summarized in a letter of April 29, 1924 from executive vice president D. Knickerbocker Boyd to Franklin D. Roosevelt, "to call attention to the very serious condition of affairs existing at this time." Boyd reminded FDR that the executive secretary, Dwight L. Hoopingarner, had served "practically" without pay, and that $7000 in back salary was owed to him. Boyd added, "This is not just or right and it should not be allowed to continue. He should not only be paid all back fees promptly but assured of prompt pay in the future—or the work should be stopped." Then Boyd commented that he, too, expected recompense for the time expended on council work, noting that time expended to date amounted to $3168.41, in addition to traveling expenses. Boyd suggested that the council face up squarely to its responsibilities, place itself on an adequate financial footing, or dissolve. The final paragraph of Boyd's letter demonstrates the fundamental objective of those promoting the American Construction Council:

> If the Council should go out of existence it would, in my opinion, be a country-wide calamity—as I doubt whether after this second effort to nationalize the great building industry on human lines, enough people with the enthusiasm, faith and patience could be found to make a third attempt.

Franklin D. Roosevelt, president of American Construction Council, had argued for "economic planning;" now the executive vice president acknowledges an "effort to nationalize" the construction industry. This effort to organize the construction industry under the somnolent eye of the government, statedly for the public good, failed.

CHAPTER 8

Wall Street Buys The New Deal

B.M. [Bernard Baruch] played a more effective role. Headquarters just didn't have any money. Sometimes they couldn't even pay the radio bill for the candidate's speeches. They had practically nothing to carry on the campaign in the critical state of Maine. Every time a crisis came, B.M. either gave the necessary money, or went out and got it.

Hugh S. Johnson, The Blue Eagle from Egg to Earth (New York: Doubleday, Doran, 1935), p. 141. On FDR's campaign in 1932.

The 1928 Presidential campaign matched Governor Alfred E. Smith, a Catholic with backing from Tammany Hall and a collectivist coloring to his politicking, against Herbert Hoover, a Quaker with a professed leaning to traditional American individualism and self-help. Herbert Hoover won by 21,392,000 votes to Smith's 15,016,000.

Where did the Wall Street banker-philosophers place their support and influence in the Smith-Hoover election? On the basis of the accepted interpretation of the philosophy of financiers, their support should have gone to Herbert Hoover. Hoover promoted the dearly beloved trade associations, dearly loved, that is, by the financial and business community. Further, in *American Individualism*[1] Herbert

1. New York: Doubleday, Page, 1922.

106

Hoover made it clear that the ideal system for America was, in his own words, "no system of laissez-faire" but, on the contrary, a regulated economy. On the other hand, the most vocally political member of the Wall Street financial establishment in 1928 was John J. Raskob, vice president of Du Pont and of General Motors and a director of Bankers Trust Co. and the County Trust Co. At the personal insistence of Governor Al Smith, Raskob became chairman of the Finance Committee of the Democratic Party. Raskob was also the largest single contributor, giving more than $350,000 to the campaign. What were the policy objectives sought by Raskob and his allies that made Al Smith so attractive a candidate?

In 1928 the key elements of what became the National Recovery program were given a public airing by John J. Raskob, Bernard Baruch, and other Wall Streeters. The promotion of Roosevelt's NRA actually dates from the 1928 Raskob speeches made in the Al Smith Presidential campaign. Although both Al Smith and Herbert Hoover depended heavily on Wall Street's "golden circle" for election funds, as we shall detail later in this chapter, the Du Pont–Raskob–Baruch money was heavily on Al Smith.

Smith, of course, lost the 1928 election for the Democrats, and Herbert Hoover became the Republican President. In spite of luke-warm Wall Street treatment, Hoover appointed many Wall Streeters to his committees and boards. Then in mid-1932, given the blunt choice between a National Recovery program in the form of the Swope Plan or less fascist policies, Hoover declined to institute corporate socialism, identified the Swope Plan for what it was, and brought the wrath of Wall Street down upon his head.

Consequently, we can trace and will trace in this chapter the Baruch proposals for NRA and the financial backing of the two Presidential candidates in each election by Raskob, Baruch, Du Pont, Rockefeller, and others of the financial élite. The main backing in each case went to the Democratic candidate willing to promote corporate socialism. In 1928 this was Al Smith, who was also a director of the Morgan-controlled Metropolitan Life Insurance Company; in 1930 it went to Roosevelt with the early bird preconvention contributions for the 1932 Hoover-Roosevelt contest. This was followed in mid-1932 by withdrawal of a great deal of Wall Street support from Herbert Hoover and the wholesale transfer of influence and money toward the election of Roosevelt.

Subsequently, FDR did not abandon his backers. The National Recovery Act with its built-in ability to coerce small business was promised and in June 1933 became law. Let's look then more closely at these events and the related evidence.

BERNARD BARUCH'S INFLUENCE ON FDR

According to his own statements Hugh Johnson, the Administrator of Roosevelt's NRA, went through a training program in the 1920s under Bernard Baruch's tutelage. Johnson records this experience as follows:

> I doubt if anybody had any more direct or complete access to sources of information than B.M. and he always gave me a free hand in the consultation and use of such scientists and experts as I might need. I was for several years the only Research Staff which he permanently maintained. That and what went before was a great training for service in NRA because these studies covered a considerable segment of the whole of American industry and the experience with government linked the two together.[2]

Johnson himself views the Raskob speeches of September and October 1928 in the Al Smith campaign as the start of Roosevelt's NRA: "There was nothing particularly new in the essence or principles developed. We had worked out and expressed precisely the same philosophy in Al Smith's campaign in 1928. . . ."[3]

Al Smith, the 1928 Democratic Presidential candidate was, as we have noted, a director of Metropolitan Life Insurance, the largest life insurance company in the U.S. and controlled by J.P. Morgan, and the greater part of his campaign funds came from the golden circle in Wall Street. Bernard Baruch outlined the NRA plan itself on May 1, 1930— an auspicious day for a socialist measure—in a speech at Boston. The content of NRA was all there, the regulation, codes, enforcement, and the carrot of welfare for the workers. It was repeated in Baruch's platform of June 1932—the one that Herbert Hoover refused to adopt. The NRA was presented again by Baruch in testimony before the Senate and in speeches before the Brookings Institution and at Johns Hopkins University. In all, Hugh Johnson counts ten documents and speeches, all presented before the election of Roosevelt in 1932, in which "will be found the development of the economic philosophy of the 1928 campaign and of almost all that happened since. Of a part of this philosophy NRA was a concrete expression."[4]

The following extracts from Baruch's May 1, 1930 speech contain the core of his proposals:

> *What business needs is a common forum where problems requiring cooperation can be considered and acted upon with the constructive, non-*

2. Hugh S. Johnson, *The Blue Eagle from Egg to Earth* (New York: Doubleday, Doran, 1935), p. 116.
3. *Ibid.*, p. 141.
4. *Ibid.*, p. 157

political sanction of government. It may have been sound public policy to forbid by law anything that looked to regulation of production when the world was in fear of famine but *it is public lunacy to decree unlimited operation of a system which periodically disgorges indigestible masses of unconsumable products. No repressive, inquisitorial, mediocre bureau will answer*—we must have a new concept for this purpose—a tribunal invested like the Supreme Court, with so much prestige and dignity that our greatest business leaders will be glad to divest themselves of all personal interest in business and there serve. Like the Supreme Court also it must be absolutely non-political.

It should have no power to repress or coerce but it should have power to convoke conference, to suggest and to sanction or license such commonsense cooperation among industrial units as will prevent our economic blessings from becoming unbearable burdens. Its sole punitive power should be to prescribe conditions of its licenses and then to revoke those licenses for infringement of such conditions.

Its deliberations should be in the open and should be wholly scientific, briefed like an engineer's report, and published to the world. Such a system would safeguard the public interest and should be substituted for the blind inhibitory blankets of the Sherman and Clayton Acts....

It is not government in business in the sense which is here condemned. *It is only a relaxation of the grip government has already taken on business by the Anti-Trust Acts. There is no fallacy in restricting ruinous excess production*—a policy which the Federal Government is now vigorously urging on Agriculture. Yet if there is nothing in the change of concept from bureaucratic precedent to that of an open forum where business can practice group self-government, acting on its own motion *under sanction of non-political, constructive and helpful tribunal* —then the idea is not practicable. *But that there is a possibility of such industrial self-government under governmental sanction was clearly demonstrated in 1918.* Many difficulties suggest themselves. In the first place anything done in the elation and fervor of war must be accepted as a criterion only with caution.

In the regulation of production price is one consideration. That is a subject which is loaded with dynamite.

There are other obvious reservations. *The thought* is revived at this critical moment because it seems worthy of consideration as an aid in a threatening economic development 'of unusual extent' and as an alternative to governmental interference and vast extension of political powers in the economic field—an eventuality which, in the absence of constructive action by business itself, is almost as certain as death and taxes.[5]

Baruch wanted by his own words a resurrection of the trade associations, relaxation of anti-trust laws, and control of business leaders and casts the reader back to the War Industries Board of 1918. To be sure, Baruch suggests "no power to coerce" and "open" deliberations, but such protestations of good faith carry small weight in the light of economic history and past furious efforts to establish cartels and com-

5. *Ibid.*, pp. 156-7. Italics in original.

binations in restraint of trade by this same group. It was to further this end that financial support for both Democrats and Republican candidates was forthcoming; the greater part of the financing originated in a relatively small geographical area of New York.

WALL STREET FINANCES THE 1928 PRESIDENTIAL CAMPAIGN

The direction of political support can be measured and identified by related financial support. The origins of the financial contributions to the Smith and Hoover campaigns of 1928 can be identified, and we find, contrary to prevailing beliefs, that it was the Democrats who received the lion's share of funds from Wall Street; as we have seen, it was in the Democratic campaign that the outlines of the National Recovery Act were first promulgated by Baruch and Raskob.

After the 1928 Presidential election the Steiwer Committee of the U.S. House of Representatives investigated the sources of campaign funds funneled into the election.[6] The detailed information was published, but the Steiwer Committee did not probe into the corporate origins and affiliations of the contributors: it merely listed names and amounts contributed. Table XIII in the report is entitled "Persons contributing sums of $5,000 and over in behalf of Republican presidential candidate." The Republican Presidential candidate was, of course, Herbert Hoover. This table lists full names and the amounts contributed, but without the affiliation of the contributors. Similarly, Table XIV of the report is entitled "Persons contributing sums of $5,000 and over in behalf of Democratic presidential candidate." Again, full names and amounts are given, but the affiliations of the person are not stated.

These lists were taken and matched by the author to the *Directory of Directors in the City of New York 1929-1930*.[7] Where the contributor as listed by the Steiwer Committee was identified as having an address within a one-mile circle of 120 Broadway in New York, the name and amount contributed were noted. No notation was made of persons not in the directory and most probably resident outside of New York City,

6. United States Congress, Senate Special Committee investigating Presidential campaign expenditures, *Presidential Campaign Expenditures. Report Pursuant to S. Res. 234, February 25 (Calendar Day, February 28),*1929. 70th Congress, 2nd session. Senate Rept. 2024 (Washington: Government Printing Office, 1929). Cited hereafter as Steiwer Committee Report.
7. New York: Directory of Directors Co., 1929.

but a record was kept of the sums of money contributed by the non-New York residents. In other words, two totals were constructed from the Steiwer Committee data: (1) contributions from persons listed as directors of companies headquartered in New York and (2) contributions from all other persons. In addition, a list of names of the New York contributors was compiled. In practice, the research procedure was biased *against* inclusion of the New York-based directors. For example, in the Democratic Party list Van-Lear Black was listed by the author as a non-New York resident, although Black was chairman of the Fidelity & Casualty Co; the company had offices at 120 Broadway, and Franklin D. Roosevelt was their New York vice president in the early 1920s. However, Black was based in Baltimore and therefore not counted as a New York director. Again Rudolph Spreckels, the sugar millionnaire, was listed in the Steiwer Committee report for a $15,000 contribution, but is not listed in the New York total, as he did not base himself in New York. Similarly, James Byrne contributed $6500 to the Smith for President campaign, but is not listed as a New York director —he was a director of the Fulton Savings Bank in Brooklyn and outside the one-mile circle. Jesse Jones, the Texas banker, contributed $20,000, but is not listed as a New York director because he was a Texas, not a New York, banker. In other words, the definition of a Wall Street contributor was very tightly and consistently drawn.

Major Wall Street Contributors to the Al Smith For President Campaign—1928

Name	Contributions			
	1924 deficit	1928 campaign	1928 deficit	Total contribution
John J. Raskob (Du Pont and General Motors)	—	$110,000	$250,000	$360,000
William F. Kenny (W.A. Harriman)	$25,000	$100,000	$150,000	$275,000
Herbert H. Lehman	$10,000	$100,000	$150,000	$260,000
M.J. Meehan (120 Broadway)	—	$50,000	$100,000	$150,000

Total $1,045,000

Source: Adapted from Louise Overacker, *Money in Elections* (New York: Macmillan, 1932), p. 155.

111

Under this restricted definition the total amount contributed by Wall Street directors, mostly connected with major banks, to the Al Smith 1928 Presidential campaign was $1,864,339. The total amount contributed by persons *not* within this golden circle was $500,531, which makes a grand total of $2,364,870. In brief, the percentage of the Al Smith for President campaign funds coming from persons giving more than $5000 and also identified as Wall Street directors was 78.83 per cent. The percentage from donors outside the golden circle was a mere 21.17 per cent. Looking at the total Al Smith contributors another way, the large contributors (over $5000) to the Smith campaign, those in the best position to ask and receive political favors, put up almost four dollars out of five.

The identity of the larger contributors to both the Al Smith campaign and the Democratic National Committee fund is listed in the attached tables.

Contributors of $25,000 or More to Democratic National Committee January to December 1928 (including contributions listed in previous table)

			NOTE
Herbert H. Lehman and Edith A. Lehman	Lehman Brothers, and Studebaker Corp.	$135,000	FDR's chief political adviser
John J. Raskob	Vice president of DuPont and General Motors	$110,000	NRA administrator
Thomas F. Ryan	President, Bankers Mortgage Co., Houston	$75,000	Chairman, Reconstruction Finance Corp.
Harry Payne Whitney	Guaranty Trust	$50,000	See Chap. 10: "The Butler Affair"
Pierre S. Du Pont	Du Pont Company, General Motors	$50,000	See Chapter 10: "The Butler Affair"
Bernard M. Baruch	Financier, 120 Broadway	$37,590	NRA planner
Robert Sterling Clark	Singer Sewing Machine Co.	$35,000	See Chap. 10: "The Butler Affair"
John D. Ryan	National City Bank, Anaconda Copper	$27,000	—
William H. Woodin	General Motors	$25,000	Secretary of Treasury, 1932

Source: Steiwer Committee Report, op. cit.

Contributions to the Democratic Presidential Primary 1928 by Directors* of the County Trust Company.

Name of Director	Contribution to Campaign and Deficit	Other Affiliations
Vincent Astor	$ 10,000	Director, Great Northern Railway, U.S. Trust Co. Trustee, N.Y. Public Library Metropolitan Opera
Howard S. Cullman	$ 6,500	Vice President, Cullman Brothers, Inc.
William J. Fitzgerald	$ 6,000	—
Edward J. Kelly	$ 6,000	—
William F. Kenny	$275,000°°	President and Director, William F. Kenny Co. Director, The Aviation Corp., Chrysler Corp.
Arthur Lehman	$ 14,000°°°	Partner, Lehman Brothers. Director, American International Corp., RKO Corp., Underwood-Elliott-Fisher Co.
M.J. Meehan	$150,000°°	61 Broadway
Daniel J. Mooney	$ 5,000	120 Broadway
John J. Raskob	$360,000°°	Director, American International Corp., Bankers Trust Co., Christiania Securities Co. Vice President, E.I. Du Pont de Nemours & Co. and General Motors Corp.
James J. Riordan	$10,000	—
Alfred E. Smith	—	Presidential Candidate Director: Metropolitan Life Insurance Co.
Total	$842,000	

Notes: °The following directors of County Trust Company did not contribute (according to the records): John J. Broderick, Peter J. Carey, John J. Cavanagh, William H. English, James P. Geagan, G. Le Boutillier, Ralph W. Long, John J. Pulleyn, and Parry D. Saylor.

°°Includes contributions to the campaign deficit.

°°°Excludes contributions by other members of the Lehman family to the Democratic Presidential campaign that totalled $168,000.

Looking at the names in these tables, it would be neither unkind nor unfair to say that the Democratic candidate was bought by Wall Street before the election. Moreover, Al Smith was a director of the County Trust Company, and the County Trust Company was the source of an extraordinarily large percentage of Democratic campaign funds.

HERBERT HOOVER'S ELECTION FUNDS

When we turn to Herbert Hoover's 1928 campaign, we also find a dependence on Wall Street financing, originating in the golden mile, but not nearly to the same extent as in Al Smith's campaign. Of a large donations total for Herbert Hoover of $3,521,141, about 51.4 per cent came from within this golden mile in New York and 48.6 per cent from outside the financial district.

Contributions of $25,000 or More to Republican National Committee, January to December 1928

Mellon family	Mellon National Bank	$50,000
Rockefeller family	Standard Oil	$50,000
Guggenheim family	Copper smelting	$75,000
Eugene Meyer	Federal Reserve Bank	$25,000
William Nelson Cromwell	Wall Street attorney	$25,000
Otto Kahn	Equitable Trust Company	$25,000
Mortimer Schiff	Banker	$25,000
		Total $275,000

Source: Steiwer Committee Report, op. cit.

Herbert Hoover was, of course, elected President; his relationship to the rise of corporate socialism has been misinterpreted in most academic and media sources. The bulk of liberal-oriented literature holds that Herbert Hoover was some kind of unreconstructed laissez-faire Neanderthal. But this view is rejected by Hoover's own statements: for example:

> Those who contended that during the period of my administration our economic system was one of laissez faire have little knowledge of the extent of government regulation. The economic philosophy of laissez faire, or "dog eat dog," had died in the United States forty years before,

114

when Congress passed the Interstate Commerce Commission and the Sherman Anti-Trust Acts.[8]

Murray Rothbard points out[9] that Herbert Hoover was a prominent supporter of Theodore Roosevelt's Progressive Party and, according to Rothbard, Hoover "challenged in a neo-Marxist manner, the orthodox laissez-faire view that labor is a commodity and that wages are to be governed by laws of supply and demand."[10] As Secretary of Commerce Hoover pushed for government cartelization of business and for trade associations, and his "outstanding" contribution, according to Rothbard," was to impose socialism on the radio industry," while the courts were working on a reasonable system of private property rights in radio frequencies. Rothbard explains these ventures into socialism on the grounds that Hoover "was . . . the victim of a terribly inadequate grasp of economics."[11] Indeed, Rothbard argues that Herbert Hoover was the real creator of the Roosevelt New Deal.

Although the evidence presented here suggests that Baruch and Raskob had more to do with FDR's New Deal, there is some validity to Rothbard's argument. Hoover's practical policies were not consistent. There are some pro-free market actions; there are many anti-free market actions. It seems plausible that Hoover was willing to accept a part, possibly a substnatial part, of a socialist program, but had a definite limit beyond which he was not willing to go.

During the course of the 1920s, in the years after the formation of the American Construction Council, more than 40 codes of practice compiled by trade associations were adopted. When he became President, and in spite of his early association with the A.C.C., Herbert Hoover promptly ended these industrial codes. He did this on the grounds that they were probably illegal associations to police prices and production and that no government could regulate these in the interest of the public. Then in February 1931 the U.S. Chamber of Commerce formed a group entitled the Committee on Continuity of Business and Employment under Henry I. Harriman. This committee came up with proposals very much like those of the New Deal: that production should be balanced to equal consumption, that the Sherman anti-trust laws should be modified to allow agreements in restraint of trade, that a national economic council should be set up under the auspices of the U.S. Chamber of Commerce, and that provision should be made for

8. *The Memoirs of Herbert Hoover: The Cabinet and the Presidency 1920-1923* (London: Hollis and Carter, 1952), p. 300.
9. *New Individualist Review*, Winter, 1966.
10. Ibid., p. 5.
11. Ibid., p. 10.

shorter hours in industry, for pensions, and for unemployment insurance. This was followed by yet another Hoover committee known as the Committee on Work Periods in Industry under P.W. Litchfield, president of Goodyear Tire and Rubber Company. Then still another committee under Standard Oil Company of New Jersey president Walter Teagle recommended sharing work, a proposal endorsed by the Litchfield Committee. Then came the Swope Plan in 1931 (see Appendix A). The plans were forthcoming, but Herbert Hoover did very little about them.

So, under Herbert Hoover, while big business was prolific in publicizing plans designed to modify the Sherman anti-trust act, allow self-regulation by industry, and establish codes in restraint of trade, President Herbert Hoover did nothing to encourage these ventures.

In fact, Hoover recognized the Swope Plan as a fascist measure and recorded this in his memoirs, along with the melancholy information that Wall Street gave him a choice of buying the Swope plan—fascist or not—and having their money and influence support the Roosevelt candidacy. This is how Herbert Hoover described the ultimatum from Wall Street under the heading of "Fascism comes to business—with dire consequences":

> Among the early Roosevelt fascist measures was the National Industry Recovery Act (NRA) of June 16, 1933. The origins of this scheme are worth repeating. These ideas were first suggested by Gerard Swope (of the General Electric Company) at a meeting of the electrical industry in the winter of 1932. Following this, they were adopted by the United States Chamber of Commerce. During the campaign of 1932, Henry I. Harriman, president of that body, urged that I agree to support these proposals, informing me that Mr. Roosevelt had agreed to do so. I tried to show him that this stuff was pure fascism; that it was merely a remaking of Mussolini's "corporate state" and refused to agree to any of it. He informed me that in view of my attitude, the business world would support Roosevelt with money and influence. That for the most part, proved true.[12]

WALL STREET BACKS FDR FOR GOVERNOR OF NEW YORK

The chief fund raiser in FDR's 1930 reelection campaign was Howard Cullman, Commissioner of the Port of New York and a director of the County Trust Company. Freidel[13] lists the campaign contributors in 1930 without their corporate affiliations. When we identify the corpo-

---

12. Herbert Hoover, *The Memoirs of Herbert Hoover: The Great Depression 1929-1941* (New York: Macmillan, 1952), p. 420.
13. Freidel, *The Ordeal,* op. cit., p. 159.

rate affiliations of these contributors, we find once again that County Trust Company of 97 Eighth Avenue, New York had an extraordinarily large interest in FDR's reelection. Apart from Howard Cullman, the following major contributors to FDR's campaign were also directors of the County Trust Company: Alfred Lehman, Alfred (Al) E. Smith, Vincent Astor, and John Raskob. Another director was FDR's old friend Dan Riordan, a customer from Fidelity & Deposit days at 120 Broadway, and William F. Kenny, yet another FDR supporter and director of County Trust. To place this list in focus, we must remember that Freidel lists 16 persons as major contributors to this campaign, and of this 16 we can identify no less than five as directors of County Trust and two other unlisted directors as known FDR supporters. Other prominent Wall Streeters financing FDR's 1930 campaign were the Morgenthau family (with the Lehmans, the heaviest contributors); Gordon Rentschler, president of the National City Bank and director of the International Banking Corporation; Cleveland Dodge, director of the National City Bank and the Bank of New York; Caspar Whitney; August Heckscher of the Empire Trust Company (120 Broadway); Nathan S. Jones of Manufacturers Trust Company; William Woodin of Remington Arms Company; Ralph Pulitzer; and the Warburg family. In brief, in the 1930 campaign the bulk of FDR's financial backing came from Wall Street bankers.

Contributors to the Pre Convention Expenses of FDR ($3,500 and Over)

Edward Flynn	$21,500	Director of Bronx County Safe Deposit Co.
W.H. Woodin	$20,000	Federal Reserve Bank of New York, Remington Arms Co.
Frank C. Walker	$15,000	
Joseph Kennedy	$10,000	Boston financier
Lawrence A. Steinhardt	$ 8,500	Member of Guggenheim, Untermeyer & Marshall, 120 Broadway
Henry Morgenthau	$ 8,000	Underwood-Elliott-Fisher
F.J. Matchette	$ 6,000	
Lehman family	$ 6,000	Lehman Brothers, 16 William Street

Dave H. Morris	$ 5,000	Director of several Wall Street firms
Sara Roosevelt	$ 5,000	
Guy P. Helvering	$ 4,500	
H.M. Warner	$ 4,500	Director, Motion Picture Producers & Distributors of America
James W. Gerard	$ 3,500	Financier, 57 William Street
Total	$117,500	

Shortly after FDR's reelection in 1930, these backers started to raise funds for the 1932 Presidential campaign. These "early bird" pre-convention contributions have been described by Flynn: "These contributors, who helped early when the need was great, so thoroughly won Roosevelt's devotion that in most instances they ultimately received substantial returns in public offices and honors."[14]

WALL STREET ELECTS FDR IN 1932

In 1932 Bernard Baruch was the key operator working behind the scenes—and sometimes not so much behind the scenes—to elect FDR, with the money and influence of big business (see epigraph to this chapter). Further, Bernard Baruch and Hugh Johnson collected numerous statistics and materials over the 1920s decade supporting their concept of national economic planning through trade associations. Johnson recounts how this information became available to FDR's speech writers. During the Roosevelt campaign of 1932:

> Ray Moley and Rex Tugwell came up to B.M.'s house and we went over all the material that B.M. and I had collected and summarized in our years of work. They, with Adolph Berle, had long before worked out the subjects of what they thought would be an ideal scheme of economic speeches for a Presidential candidate, but they had few facts. From that moment we joined Ray Moley's forces and we all went to work to find for Franklin Roosevelt the data which he welded into the very remarkable series of simply expressed speeches on homely economics which convinced this country that here was the leader upon whom it could rely.[15]

In rereading the FDR campaign speeches, it becomes obvious that

14. John T. Flynn, "Whose Child is the NRA?" *Harper's Magazine* Sept. 1932, pp. 84-5.
15. Hugh S. Johnson, *The Blue Eagle from Egg to Earth,* op. cit., pp. 140-1.

PROPORTION OF ELECTION FUNDS
FROM WALL STREET

(Defined as a one-mile circle centered on 120 Broadway, New York).

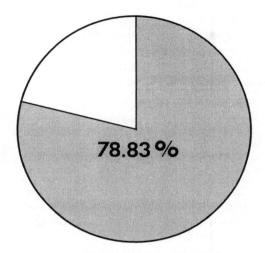

AL SMITH FOR PRESIDENT
DEMOCRATIC CAMPAIGN - 1928
(Contributions over $25,000)

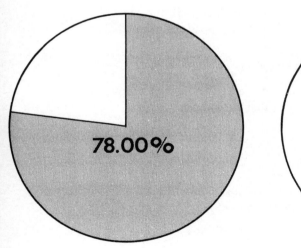

FRANKLIN D. ROOSEVELT: 1932
PRE CONVENTION EXPENSES
(Contributions over $3500)

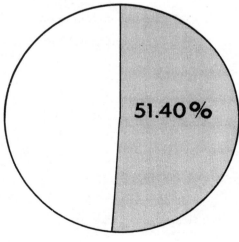

HERBERT HOOVER FOR PRESIDENT
REPUBLICAN CAMPAIGN - 1928
(Contributions over $25,000)

they lack concreteness and specific facts. Presumably the Moley-Tug-well team set out the general theme and Baruch and Johnson intro-duced supporting statements in such areas as credit expansion, the consequences of speculation, the role of the Federal Reserve system, and so on. It is remarkable, but perhaps not surprising, that these Baruch-influenced speeches took the reader back to World War I, cited the contemporary emergency as greater than that of the war, and then subtly suggested similar Baruchian solutions. For example, at the Jef-ferson Day Dinner speech of April 18, 1932 Roosevelt said, or was prompted to say:

> Compare this panic stricken policy of delay and inprovization with that devised to meet the emergency of war fifteen years ago. We met specific situations with considered, relevant measures of constructive value. There were the War Industries Board, the Food and Fuel Administration, the War Trade Board, the Shipping Board and many others.[16]

Then in May 22, 1932 Roosevelt addressed himself to the theme "The Country Needs, the Country Demands, Persistent Experimenta-tion" and called for national economic planning. This speech was followed on July 2, 1932 by the first hint of the New Deal. Finally, in accepting the nomination for the Presidency at Chicago, FDR said "I pledge you—I pledge myself to a New Deal for the American People."

Note

Freidel's list of preconvention contributors to Franklin Delano Roosevelt's 1932 Presidential campaign.

1932 Preconvention Contributors[17]

(over $2,000)	Affiliations
James W. Gerard	Laughton, Gerard, Bowen & Halpin (see Julian A. Gerard)
Guy Helvering	
Col. E.M. House New York	
Joseph P. Kennedy 1560 Broadway	Ambassador to Court of St. James New England Fuel & Transportation Co.
Henry Morgenthau, Sr. 1133 Fifth Avenue	Underwood-Elliott-Fisher

16. *The Public Papers and Addresses of Franklin D. Roosevelt;* Vol. 1, *The Genesis of the New Deal, 1928-1932* (New York: Random House, 1938), p. 632.
17. Freidel, *The Ordeal,* op. cit., p. 172.

Dave Hennen Morris	Bank of N.Y. & Trust Co. (Asst. Comptroller); American Savings Bank (Trustee)
Mrs. Sara Delano Roosevelt Hyde Park, N.Y.	FDR's mother
Laurence A. Steinhardt 120 Broadway	Guggenheim, Untermeyer & Marshall
Harry M. Warner 321 W. 44th St.	Motion Picture Producers & Distributors of America, Inc.
William H. Woodin Secretary of the Treasury	American Car & Foundry; Remington Arms Co.
Edward J. Flynn 529 Courtlandt Ave.	Bronx County Safe Deposit Co.

James A. Farley adds to this list:

William A. Julian	Director, Central Trust Co.
Jesse I. Straus 1317 Broadway	President, R.H. Macy & Co. N.Y. Life Insurance
Robert W. Bingham	Publisher, Louisville *Courier-Journal*
Basil O'Connor 120 Broadway	FDR's law partner

121

PART III

FDR AND THE
CORPORATE SOCIALISTS

CHAPTER 9

The Swope Plan

I think this is as revolutionary as anything that happened in this country in 1776, or in France in 1789, or in Italy under Mussolini or in Russia under Stalin.
Senator Thomas P. Gore in the National Recovery Administration Hearings, U.S. Senate Finance Committee, May 22, 1933.

Although the New Deal and its most significant component, the National Recovery Administration (NRA), are generally presented as the progeny of FDR's brain trust, as we have seen the essential principles had been worked out in detail long before FDR and his associates came to power. The FDR group did little more than put the stamp of academic approval to an already prepared plan.

The roots of the Roosevelt NRA are of peculiar importance. As we have seen in Chapter 6, allowing for vast changes in the industrial structure, NRA approximated a schema worked out in 1841 by FDR's ancestor, Assemblyman Clinton Roosevelt of New York. Then we noted that wartime dictator Bernard Baruch was preparing an NRA-like program in the 1920s and that he and his assistant Hugh Johnson were very much an integral part of the preliminary planning. Further, the Roosevelt NRA was in its details a plan presented by Gerard Swope (1872-1957) long-time president of General Electric Company. This

Swope Plan[1] was in turn comparable to a German plan worked out in World War I by his opposite number Walter Rathenau, head of German General Electric (Allgemeine Elektizitäts Gesellschaft) in Germany, where it was known as the Rathenau Plan. So let's take a closer look at the Swope Plan.

THE SWOPE FAMILY

The Swope family was of German origin. In 1857 Isaac Swope, a German immigrant, settled in St. Louis as a manufacturer of watch cases. Two of Swope's sons, Herbert Bayard Swope and Gerard Swope, subsequently rose to the peak of American enterprise. Herbert Bayard Swope was long-time editor of the New York *World*, a racetrack devotee, a close friend of Bernard Baruch, and used by FDR as an unofficial envoy during the New Deal period. Herbert's brother Gerard made his career with General Electric Company. Swope started as a helper on the factory floor in 1893, became a sales representative in 1899, manager of the St. Louis office in 1901, and director of the Western Electric Company in 1913. During World War I Swope was assistant director of purchase, storage, and traffic in the Federal government under General George W. Goethals and planned the U.S. Army procurement program. In 1919 Swope became the first president of the International General Electric Company. Successful promotion of G.E.'s foreign business brought him to the presidency of G.E. in 1922 to succeed Edwin Rice, Jr. Swope remained as G.E.'s president from 1922 until 1939.

General Electric was a Morgan-controlled company and always had one or two Morgan partners on its board, while Swope was also a director of other Wall Street enterprises, including International Power Securities Co. and the National City Bank.

Gerard Swope's political development began in the 1890s. Biographer David Loth reports that, soon after coming to Chicago, Swope was introduced to socialists Jane Addams, Ellen Gates Starr, and their Hull House Settlement. This interest in social affairs developed to culminate in the 1931 Swope plan for stabilization of industry, 90 per cent of which consisted of a scheme for workmen's compensation, life and disability insurance, old-age pensions, and unemployment protection. The Swope plan is an extraordinary document. One short paragraph removes all industry from the anti-trust laws—a long-time industrial goal—while numerous lengthy paragraphs detail proposed

---

1. See Appendix A for the full text.

social plans. In sum, the Swope Plan was a transparent device to lay the groundwork for the corporate state by defusing potential labor opposition with a massive welfare carrot.

The Swope Plan and Bernard Baruch's earlier and similar proposal became the Roosevelt National Recovery Act. The Wall Street origins of NRA did not go unnoticed when the act was debated by Congress. Witness for example, the indignant, but not altogether accurate, outburst of Senator Huey P. Long:

> I come here now and I complain. I complain in the name of the people of my country, of the sovereign State I represent. I complain in the name of the people wherever else it may be known. I complain if it be true, as I am informed by Senators on this floor, that under this act Mr. Johnson, a former employee of Mr. Baruch, has been put in charge of the administration of the act, and has already called as his aides the head of the Standard Oil Co., the head of General Motors, and the head of the General Electric Co.
>
> I complain if Mr. Peek, who is an employee of Mr. Baruch, or has been, as I have been informed on the floor of the Senate, has been placed in charge of administering the Farm Act, however good a man he may be and whatever his ideas may be.
>
> I complain if Mr. Brown, who, I am informed on the floor of the Senate, has been made an influential manipulator of the office of the Bureau of the Director of the Budget, has been an employee of Mr. Baruch, and is now given this authority. I complain because, on the 12th day of May 1932, before we went to Chicago to nominate a President of the United States, I stood in this very place on this floor and told the people of this country that we were not going to have the Baruch influence, at that time so potent with Hoover, manipulating the Democratic Party before nomination, after nomination, or after election.[2]

Huey Long was correct to point up the Wall Street dominance of NRA, but his identifications are a little haphazard. Hugh Johnson, long-time associate of Bernard Baruch, was indeed appointed head of NRA. Further, Johnson's principal assistants in NRA were three corporate heads: Walter C. Teagle, president of Standard Oil of New Jersey: Gerard Swope, president of General Electric and author of the Swope Plan; and Louis Kirstein, vice president of William Filene's Sons of Boston. As we have seen (p. 80) Filene was a long-time proponent of corporate socialism. The "head of General Motors" cited by Senator Long was Alfred P. Sloan, not related to NRA, but G.M. vice president John Raskob, who was the big fund raiser in 1928 and 1932 and behind-the-scenes operator promoting the election of Franklin D. Roosevelt in 1932. In other words, key positions in NRA and in the Roosevelt Administration itself were manned by men from Wall Street. The pub-

2. Senator Huey P. Long, *Congressional Record*, June 8, 1933, p. 5250.

lic relations explanation for business men turned bureaucrats is that businessmen have the experience and should become involved in public service. The intent in practice has been to control industry. It should not, however, surprise us if the corporate socialists go to Washington D.C. after election of their favorite sons to take over the reins of monopoly administration. One would have to be naive to think it would be otherwise after the massive election investments recorded in Chapter 8.

Before President Roosevelt was inaugurated in March 1933, a so-called brain trust was more or less informally put to work on economic plans for the Roosevelt era. This group comprised General Hugh Johnson, Bernard Baruch (see p. 106 for his political contributions), Alexander Sachs of Lehman Brothers (see p. 117 for political contributions), Rexford G. Tugwell, and Raymond Moley. This small group, three from Wall Street and two academics, generated Roosevelt's economic planning.

This link between Bernard Baruch and NRA planning has been recorded by Charles Roos in his definitive volume on NRA:

> Early in March 1933 Johnson and Baruch started on a hunting trip and en route stopped in Washington. Moley had dinner with them and proposed that Johnson remain in Washington to draft a plan for industrial recovery. . . . The idea appealed to Baruch, and he promptly granted Johnson leave of absence from his regular duties. Then Johnson and Moley, after some study of the various proposals believed by the latter to have merit, proceeded to draw up a bill which would organize industry in an attack on the depression.[3]

According to Roos, Johnson's first NRA draft was on two sheets of foolscap paper and provided simply for suspension of the anti-trust laws, together with almost unlimited authority for President Roosevelt to do almost anything he wished with the economy, including licensing and control of industry. According to Roos, "It was, of course, rejected by the Administration, since it would have made the President a dictator, and such power was not desired."

This seemingly incidental rejection of unwanted dictatorial power by the Roosevelt administration may be of some significance. In Chapter 10 we will describe the Butler affair, an attempt by the same Wall Street interests to install Roosevelt as a dictator or replace him with a more pliant figurehead in case of his objection. Johnson's first draft attempts were to set up NRA in a form consistent with Roosevelt as an economic dictator, and its rejection by Roosevelt is consistent with serious charges laid at the feet of Wall Street (p. 141). At this point in

3. Charles F. Ross, *NRA Economic Planning* (Indianapolis: The Principia Press, 1937), p. 37.

the planning, according to Roos, Johnson and Moley were joined by Tugwell and later by Donald R. Richberg, a Chicago labor attorney. The three proceeded to draft a more "comprehensive" bill, whatever that meant.

General Hugh Johnson, was appointed head of the National Recovery Administration created under the title of the N.I.R.A. and believed for a while that he was also to head the Public Works Administration. The plans and diagrams drawn up by General Johnson and Alexander Sachs of Lehman Brothers assumed that the NRA head would also direct the public works program.

Consequently, we can find the roots of the NRA bill and the Public Works Administration in this small Wall Street group. Their effort reflects both the Swope and the Baruch plans for corporate socialism, with an initial attempt to provide for a corporate dictatorship in the United States.

SOCIALIST PLANNERS OF THE 1930s

There were, of course, many other plans in the early 1930s; indeed, economic planning was endemic among the academics, politicians, and businessmen of this era. The weight of informed opinion considered economic planning essential to raise America from the depression. Those who doubted the efficacy and wisdom of economic planning were few and far between. Unfortunately, in the early 1930s no empiric experience existed to demonstrate that economic planning is inefficient, creates more problems than it solves, and leads to loss of individual freedom. To be sure, Ludwig von Mises had written *Socialism* and made his accurate predictions on the chaos of planning, but von Mises was even then an unknown economic theoretician. There is a mystical lure to economic planning. Its proponents always implicitely visualize *themselves* as the planners, and the anticapitalist psychology, so well described by von Mises, is the psychological pressure behind the scenes to make the plan come about. Even today in 1975, long after economic planning has been totally discredited, we still have the siren song of prosperity by planning. J. Kenneth Galbraith is one prominently vocal example, no doubt because Galbraith's personal estimate of his abilities and wisdom is greater than that of America at large. Galbraith recognizes that planning offers a means to exercise his assumed abilities to the full. The rest of us are to be coerced into the plan by the police power of the state: a negation of liberal principles perhaps, but logic was never a strong point among the economic engineers.

In any case, in the 1930s economic planning had many more enthusiastic proponents and far fewer critics than today. Almost everyone was a Galbraith, and the basic content of the plans proposed was notably similar to his. The table below lists the more prominent plans and their outstanding attributes. Industry, always anxious to find shelter from competition in the police power of the state, itself proposed three plans. The most important of these industry plans, the Swope plan, had compulsory features for all companies with more than 50 employees, combining continuous regulation with, as we have noted, extraordinarily costly welfare proposals. The Swope plan is reproduced in full as Appendix A; the full text reflects the lack of well-thought-out administrative proposals and the preponderance of irresponsible give-away welfare features. The first few paragraphs of the plan give the core of Swope's proposals: trade associations, enforced by the state and with power of enforcement concentrated in the hands of major corporations through a system of industrial votes. While 90 per cent of the proposal text is devoted to give-away pensions for workers, unemployment insurance, life insurance and so on, the core is in the first few paragraphs. In brief, the Swope Plan was a carrot to get what Wall Street so earnestly desired: monopoly trade associations with the ability to use state power to enforce monopoly—Frederic Howe's maxim of "get society to work for you" in practice.

Economic Stabilization Plans: 1933

Name of Plan	Proposal for Industry	Government Regulation	Welfare Proposals
Industry Plans			
Swope Plan (General Electric)	Trade Associations, membership compulsory after three years for companies with 50 or more employees. Rulings mandatory	Continuous regulation by Federal Trade Commission	Life and disability insurance, pensions, and unemployment insurance
U.S. Chamber of Commerce Plan	National Economic Council; power not mandatory	No regulation	Individual corporation plans; public works planning

Associated General Contractors of America Plan	Grant by Congress of greater power to Federal Reserve Board. Bond issues to be authorized for revolving fund for construction; bond for increasing public and semi-public construction. Federal Reserve to guarantee solvency of banks	Financial regulation. Licensing of contractors. Establishment of construction credit bureaus	Stimulation of employment through greater building and construction activity. State bonds for public buildings; development of home loan banks

Labor Plans

American Federation of Labor Plan	National Economic Council; power not mandatory	No regulation	Spread jobs; maintenance of wages; guarantees of jobs; long-range stabilization plans. Five-day week and shorter day immediately. Program of public building

Academic and General

Stuart Chase Plan	Revival of War Industries Board using coercive, mandatory power, confined to 20 or 30 basic industries	Continuous regulation	National employment bureaus; reduction of hours; unemployment insurance; raising of wages; allocation of labor
National Civic Federation Plan	"Business Congress" of industrial organizations. No limitations or restrictions; full and complete power to fix prices or combine	Continuous regulation	Unemployment insurance plan. Raise wages

| Beard Plan | "National Economic Council," authorized by Congress, to coordinate finance, operation, distribution, and public service enterprises. Each industry governed by subsidiary syndicates | Continuous regulation | Use of unemployed on housing and public project programs |

The U.S. Chamber of Commerce plan was similar to the Swope plan, but required only voluntary compliance with the code and did not embody the extensive welfare clauses of the Swope plan. The Chamber of Commerce plan was also based on voluntary compliance, not the coercive government regulation inherent in the Swope proposal.

The third industry plan was put forward by the Associated General Contractors of America. The AGC plan proposed that greater powers be granted the Federal Reserve System to guarantee banks bonds for public construction and, not surprisingly, establishment of special construction credit bureaus financed by the state, coupled with licensing of contractors. In brief, the AGC wanted to keep out competition and tap Federal (taxpayers') funds for promotion of the construction industry.

The American Federation of Labor plan proposed a National Economic Council to spread and guarantee jobs and embark on economic planning for stabilization. The unions did not push for government regulation.

The academic plans were notable in the sense that they supported industry objectives. Stuart Chase, a well-known socialist, came up with something very close to the Wall Street plans: in effect, a revival of Bernard Baruch's 1918 War Industries Board, with coercive power granted to industry, but confined to 20 or 30 basic industries, with continuous regulation. The Chase plan was an approximation of Italian fascism. The Beard plan also proposed syndicates along Italian lines, with continuous regulation and use of the unemployed in public programs á la Marx and *The Communist Manifesto*. The National Civic Federation advocated the total planning concept: full and complete power to fix prices and combinations, with state regulation and welfare features to appease labor.

Almost no one, except of course Ludwig von Mises, pointed to the roots of the problem to draw the logical conclusion from economic history that the best economic planning is no economic planning.[4]

SOCIALISTS GREET THE SWOPE PLAN

Orthodox socialists greeted Swope's plan with a curious, if perhaps understandable, restraint. On the one hand, said the socialists, Swope had recognized the evils of unrestrained capitalism. On the other hand the Swope system, complained the socialists, would leave control of industry in the hands of industry itself rather than to the state. As Norman Thomas explained:

> Mr. Swope's scheme of regulation is a probably unconstitutional plan for putting the power of government behind the formation of strong capitalist syndicates which will seek to control the government which regulates them and, failing that, will fight it.[5]

Socialist criticism of General Electric's Swope did not consider whether the Swope system would work or had operational efficiency or how it proposed to work; orthodox socialist criticism was limited to the observation that control would be in the wrong hands if industry took over and not in the right hands of the government planners, that is, the socialists themselves. In sum, the dispute was over who was going to control the economy: Mr. Gerard Swope or Mr. Norman Thomas.

Consequently, the Thomas criticism of Swope has a curious duality, sometimes praiseful:

> Certainly it is significant that at least one of our authentic captains of industry, one of the real rulers of America, has overcome the profound and bewildered reluctance of the high and mighty to go beyond the sorriest platitudes in telling us how to break the depression they did so much to cause and so little to avert. Obviously Mr. Swope's speech had its good points . . . [6]

At other times Thomas is skeptical and points out that Swope, ". . . no longer trusts individual initiative, competition and the automatic working of markets," but proposes to gear the system to the benefit of "the stockholding class."

There is no evidence that Gerard Swope and his associates ever trusted individual initiative, competition, and free markets any more

---

4. Should the reader wish to pursue the explanation for this pervasive inability to see the obvious, he could start in no better place than Ludwig von Mises, *The Anti-Capitalistic Mentality* (New York: Van Nostrand, 1956).
5. "A Socialist Looks at the Swope Plan," *The Nation*, Oct. 7, 1931, p. 358.
6. *Ibid.*, p. 357.

than did Norman Thomas. This is an important observation because, once we abandon the myths of all capitalists as entrepreneurs and all liberal planners as saviors of the little man, we see them both for what they are: totalitarians and the opponents of individual liberty. The only difference between them is *who* is to be the director.

THE THREE MUSKETEERS OF NRA

The National Recovery Administration, most important segment of the New Deal, was then designed, constructed, and promoted by Wall Street. In essence, the NRA originated with Bernard Baruch and his long-time assistant General Johnson. In detail, NRA was the Swope Plan, and its general principles were promoted over the years by numerous prominent Wall Streeters.

There were, of course, planning variants from the socialists and Marxist-influenced planners, but these variants were not the versions that finally became NRA. NRA was essentially fascist in that industry, not central state planners, had the authority to plan, and these industrial planners came from the New York financial establishment. Bernard Baruch's office was at 120 Broadway; the offices of Franklin D. Roosevelt (the New York offices of Fidelity & Deposit and the law offices of Roosevelt & O'Connor) were also at 120 Broadway. Gerard Swope's office and the executive offices of General Electric Company were at the same address. We can therefore say in a limited sense that the Roosevelt NRA was born at 120 Broadway, New York City.

General Hugh Johnson had three principal assistants in NRA, and "these three musketeers were on the job longer and they walked in and out of my office whenever they discovered anything that needed attention."[7] The three assistants were Wall Streeters from major industries who themselves held prominent positions in major firms in these industries: Gerard Swope, president of General Electric, Walter C. Teagle, of Standard Oil of New Jersey, and Louis Kirstein of William Filene's Sons, the retail merchants. Through this trio, a dominant element of big business was in control at the very peak of NRA. This concentration of control explains the thousands of complaints of NRA oppression that came from medium and small businessmen.

Who were these men? As we have noted, Gerard Swope of General Electric had been assistant to General Johnson in the War Industries Board of World War I. While NRA was under discussion, Johnson "suggested his name to Secretary Roper at once." General Electric was

7. Hugh S. Johnson, *The Blue Eagle from Egg to Earth*, op. *cit.*, p. 217.

in 1930 the largest of the electrical equipment manufacturers, with Westinghouse holding many of the basic patents in the field, as well as a large interest in RCA and many international subsidiaries and affiliates. In the late 1920s G.E. and Westinghouse produced about three quarters of the basic equipment for distributing and generating electric power in the U.S. General Electric, however was the dominant firm in the electrical equipment industry.[8] Under NRA the National Electrical Manufacturers Association (NEMA) was designated as the agency for supervising and administering the electrical industry code. NEMA moved promptly and by July 1933 presented the second code of "fair competition" for the President's signature.

Johnson's second musketeer was Walter Teagle, chairman of the board of the Standard Oil of New Jersey. Standard of New Jersey was the biggest integrated oil company in the U.S., and only Royal Dutch challenged it in international sales. Jersey Standard was controlled by the Rockefeller family, whose holdings in the early 1930s have been estimated at between 20 and 25 per cent.[9] One might therefore say that Teagle represented the Rockefeller interests in NRA, whereas Swope represented the Morgan interests. It is interesting to note in passing that the largest Standard competitor was Gulf Oil, controlled by the Mellon interests, and there were persistent efforts early in the Roosevelt administration to prosecute Mellon for tax evasion.

The third of Johnson's three musketeers at NRA was Louis Kirstein, vice president of Filene's of Boston. Edward Filene is notable for his books on the advantages of trade associations, fair competition, and cooperation (see page 81 below).

The peak of the Roosevelt National Recovery Administration consisted of the president of the largest electrical corporation, the chairman of the largest oil company, and the representative of the most prominent financial speculator in the United States.

In brief, the administration of NRA was a reflection of the New York financial establishment and its pecuniary interests. Further, as we have seen, since the plan itself originated in Wall Street, the presence of businessmen in the administration of NRA cannot be explained on the basis of their experience and administrative ability. NRA was a creature of Wall Street implemented by Wall Streeters.

THE OPPRESSION OF SMALL BUSINESS

The proponents of the National Industrial Recovery Act made a great

---

8. For more information see Harry W. Laidler, *Concentration of Control in American Industry* (New York: Crowell, 1931), Chapter XV.
9. *Ibid.*, p. 20.

show that NRA would protect the small businessman who, it was alleged, had suffered in the past from unfair application of the anti-trust laws; the suspension of the anti-trust laws would remove their more unwelcome features, while NRA would preserve their welcome anti-monopoly provisions. Senator Wagner stated that *all* industry would formulate the proposed industrial codes, not just big business. Senator Borah, on the contrary, contended that "monopoly" was about to receive a service it had coveted for over 25 years, that is, "the death of the antitrust laws" and that the NRA industrial codes "are going to be combinations or contracts in restraint of trade, or it would not be necessary to suspend the antitrust laws." Senator Borah also pointedly accused Senator Wagner of betraying the legitimate businessman for the sake of Wall Street:

> The elder Rockefeller did not need any criminal law to aid him when he was building up his wealth. He destroyed the independents everywhere; he scattered them to the four winds; he concentrated his great power. But the Senator would not only give to the combines all the power to write their code, but would give them the power to indict and prosecute the man who violated the code, although he might be pursuing a perfectly legitimate business.
>
> Mr. President, I do not care how much we strengthen, how much we build up, how much we buttress the antitrust law: I object to a suspension in any respect whatever, because I know that when those laws are suspended, we give these 200 nonbanking corporations, which control the wealth of the United States, a stupendous power, which can never be controlled except through the criminal laws enforced by the courts.[10]

Senator Borah then cited Adam Smith (see p. 99) to effect, pointing out that no definition of fair competition was in the bill and that codes of fair competition would degenerate into the dictates of the major corporations. Similarly, Senator Gore pointed to the possibility that the President could require all members of an industry to be licensed and that this meant that the President could revoke a license at his pleasure, an obvious infringement on due process of law and basic property rights:

> SENATOR GORE. Could the President revoke that license at this pleasure?
>
> SENATOR WAGNER. Yes, for a violation of the code imposed by the Federal Government.
>
> SENATOR GORE. On what sort of hearing?
>
> SENATOR WAGNER. After a hearing. It is provided that a hearing may be had, before a license can be revoked.
>
> SENATOR GORE. That is something that really affects the life and death of a particular industry or enterprise, if he has the power to revoke the license.

10. *Congressional Record,* 1933, p. 5165.

SENATOR WAGNER. Yes; it is a sanction.

SENATOR GORE. What I wanted to ask you, Senator, is this: Do you think you could place that power in the hands of an executive officer?

SENATOR WAGNER. I do, in the case of an emergency.

SENATOR GORE. To exterminate an industry?

SENATOR WAGNER. All of these powers, of course, are lodged in one individual, and we have just got to rely upon him to administer it fairly and justly. We had the same sort of power during the war.

SENATOR GORE. I know that, and Mr. Hoover, if I may use these words, put free-born American citizens out of business without trial by jury.

SENATOR WAGNER. The philosophy of this bill is to encourage voluntary action and initiative on the part of industry, and I doubt whether or not these compulsory methods will be used at all except on very rare occasions; but if you are going to lift the standard, you have got to have some sanctions in order to enforce the code that may be adopted.

SENATOR GORE. I understand, but if you are going to carry out this system you have to have power to carry it out. My point is why in a free country a free man ought to be required to take out a license to engage in legitimate industry, and why somebody under our constitutional system should be given the power to destroy the value of his property, which you do when you bring about a situation where he cannot operate. That seems to me approaching the point of taking property without due process of law.[11]

When we examine the results of the N.I.R.A., even a few short months after passage of the bill, we find that these Senatorial fears were fully justified and that President Roosevelt had abandoned the small businessman of the United States to the control of Wall Street. Many industries were dominated by a few major firms, in turn under control of Wall Street investment houses. These major firms were dominant, through the three musketeers, in establishing the NRA codes. They had the most votes and could and did set prices and conditions ruinous to smaller firms.

The iron and steel industry is a good example of the manner in which large firms dominated the NRA code. In the 1930s two leading companies, United States Steel, with 39 per cent, and Bethlehem Steel, with 13.6 per cent, controlled over half of the country's steel ingot capacity. The board of U.S. Steel included J.P. Morgan and Thomas W. Lamont, as well as chairman Myron C. Taylor. The board of Bethlehem included Percy A. Rockefeller and Grayson M-P. Murphy of Guaranty Trust, whom we shall meet again in Chapter 10.

In 1930 the largest stockholders of U.S. Steel were George F. Baker and George F. Baker, Jr., with combined shares of 2000 preferred and

11. United States Senate, *National Industrial Recovery*, Hearings before Committee on Finance, 73rd Congress, 1st Session, S.1712 and H.R. 5755 (Washington: Government Printing Office, 1933), p. 5.

107,000 common; Myron C. Taylor head of the Finance Committee of U.S. Steel owned 27,800 shares of common; J.P. Morgan held 1261 shares; and James A. Farrell had title to 4850 shares of preferred stock. These men were also substantial Presidential campaign contributors. For example, in Hoover's 1928 campaign they contributed:

J.P. Morgan	$5,000
J.P. Morgan Company	$42,500
George F. Baker	$27,000
George F. Baker Jr.	$20,000
Myron C. Taylor	$25,000

In the NRA, we find that U.S. Steel and Bethlehem Steel effectively controlled the whole industry by virtue of their votes in the industrial codes; of a total of 1428 votes, these two companies alone were allowed a total of 671 votes, or 47.2 per cent, perilously close to outright control and with undoubted ability to find an ally among the smaller but still significant companies.

NRA-Voting Strength in the Iron and Steel Industry Code

Company[12]	Votes in Code Authority	Percentage of Total
U.S. Steel	511	36.0
Bethlehem Steel	160	11.2
Republic Steel	86	6.0
National Steel	81	5.7
Jones and Laughlin	79	5.5
Youngstown Sheet & Tube	74	5.1
Wheeling Steel	73	5.1
American Rolling Mill	69	4.8
Inland Steel	51	3.6
Crucible Steel	38	2.7
McKeesport Tin Plate	27	1.9
Allegheny Steel	21	1.5
Spang-Chalfant	17	1.2
Sharon Steel Hoop	16	1.1
Continental Steel	16	1.1

Source: NRA Report *Operation of the Basing Point System in the Iron and Steel Industry.*

12. In addition, the following smaller firms had votes: Acme Steel (9), Granite City Steel (8), Babcock and Wilcox (8), Alan Wood (7), Washburn Wire (7), Interlake Iron (7), Follansbee Bros. (6), Ludlum Steel (6), Superior Steel (6), Bliss and Laughlin (6), Laclede Steel (5), Apollo Steel (5), Atlantic Steel (4), Central Iron and Steel (4), A.M.

Although U.S. Steel and Bethlehem were the major units in the iron and steel industry before passage of the NRA, they were unable to control competition from numerous smaller firms. After the passage of NIRA, these two firms were able, through their dominance of the code system, also to dominate the iron and steel industry.

John D. Rockefeller organized the Standard Oil trust in 1882 but, as a result of court orders under the Sherman Act, the cartel was dissolved into 33 independent companies. In 1933 these companies were still controlled by the Rockefeller family interests; the Sherman Act was more shadow than substance:

Company	Net income (1930) in Million $$
Standard Oil of New Jersey	57
Standard Oil of Indiana	46
Standard Oil of California	46
Standard Oil of New York	16

Offices of the "independent" Standard companies continued to be located at Rockefeller headquarters, at this time at 25 and 26 Broadway. During the 1920s new capital entered, and there was a relative shift in the importance of the various Standard Oil companies. By the time of the New Deal the largest single unit was Standard Oil of New Jersey, in which the Rockefeller interests held a 20 to 25 per cent interest. The president of New Jersey Standard, Walter S. Teagle, became one of the three musketeers of NRA.

When we look at the auto industry in 1930 we find that two companies, Ford and General Motors, sold about three quarters of the cars produced in the United States. If we include Chrysler, the three companies sold about five sixths of all U.S. automobiles produced:

Ford Motor Co. ....40 per cent
General Motors ....35 per cent
Chrysler Corp. ....8 per cent

Under its founder, Henry Ford, the Ford Motor Company had little use for politics, although James Couzens, one of the original Ford stockholders, later became Senator from Michigan. Ford maintained its executive offices in Dearborn, Michigan and only a sales office in New York. Ford was also vehemently anti-NRA and anti-Wall Street,

Byers Company (4), Sloss-Sheffield (4), Woodward Iron (3), Firth-Sterling (2), Davison Coke and Iron (2), Soullin Steel (1), Harrisburg Pipe (1), Eastern Rolling Mill (1), Michigan Steel Tube (1), Milton Manufacturing Company (1), and Cranberry Furnace (1).

and Henry Ford is notable by reason of his absence from the lists of contributors to Presidential campaigns.

On the other hand, General Motors was a creature of Wall Street. The firm was controlled by the J.P. Morgan firm; the chairman of the board was Pierre S. Du Pont, of the Du Pont Company, which in 1933 had about a 25 per cent interest in General Motors. In 1930 the General Motors board comprised Junius S. Morgan, Jr. and George Whitney of the Morgan firm; directors from the First National Bank and Bankers Trust; seven directors from Du Pont; and Owen D. Young of General Electric.

Another example is the International Harvester Company, in 1930 under its president Alexander Legge the giant of the agricultural equipment industry. Legge was part of the NRA. The agricultural equipment combination was formed in 1920 by the J.P. Morgan Company and controlled about 85 per cent of the total production of harvesting machines in the United States. In 1930, the firm was still dominant in the industry:

Company	Assets	Percentage of Market
International Harvester (11 Broadway)	$384 million (1929)	60
Deere & Co.	$107	17
J.I. Case	$55	8
Others	$100	15
Total	$646 million	100

In 1930 at least 80 large companies were mining bituminous coal in the United States; of these, two—Pittsburgh Coal and Consolidation Coal—were dominant. Pittsburgh Coal was under control of the Pittsburgh banking family, the Mellons. Consolidation Coal was largely owned by J.D. Rockefeller, who owned 72 per cent of the preferred and 28 per cent of the common stock. Both the Mellons and the Rockefellers were heavy political contributors. Similarly, anthracite production was concentrated in the hands of the Reading Railroad, which mined 44 per cent of U.S. hard coal. Reading was controlled by the Baltimore and Ohio Railroad, which held 66 per cent of its stock, and the chairman of B & O was E.T. Stotesbury, a partner in the Morgan firm.

When we look at machine-building firms in the United States in 1930, we find that the largest by far was General Electric—and president Swope of G.E. was intimately connected with NRA.

140

Major Machine Building Firms (1929)

Firm	Assets in Millions	Profits (1929) in Millions	Sales (1929) in Millions
General Electric, 120 Broadway	$500	$71	$415.3
American Radiator & Standard Sanitary, 40 W. 40th St.	226	20	
Westinghouse Electric, 150 Broadway	225	27	216.3
Baldwin Locomotive, 120 Broadway	100	3	40
American Locomotive, 30 Church St.	106	7	
American Car & Foundry, 30 Church St.	120	2.7	
International Business Machines, 50 Broadway	40	6.7	
Otis Elevator, 260 11th Avenue	57	8	
Crane Company	116	11.5	

As we glance down the list we note that American Car & Foundry (whose president, Woodin, became Secretary of the Treasury under Roosevelt), American Radiator & Standard, and Crane Company were all prominent contributors to FDR.

Given this dominant influence of large firms in the NRA and the Roosevelt administration, it is not surprising that NRA was administered in a manner oppressive to small business. Even in the brief life of NRA, until it was declared unconstitutional, we find evidence of oppression: witness the complaints by small business in the industries we have discussed compared to other industries in small business with many more units:

Industry	Numbers of Complaints of Oppression (January-April 1934)
Major Industry	
Iron and Steel	66
Investment Banking	47
Petroleum	60
Electrical Manufacturing	9

Small Business

Cleaning and Dyeing	31
Ice	12
Printing	22
Boot and Shoes	10
Laundry	9

Source: Roos, NRA Economic Planning, p. 411, from unpublished NRA data.

To sum up, we can trace the Roosevelt National Recovery Administration from planning on Wall Street to implementation by prominent financiers and industrialists with the obvious result: oppression of small business in a manner reminiscent of the Rockefeller–Morgan activities of the late 19th century.

CHAPTER 10

FDR; Man on the White Horse

In the last few weeks of the committee's official life it received evidence showing that certain persons had made an attempt to establish a fascist organization in this country. There is no question that these attempts were discussed, were planned, and might have been placed in execution when and if the financial backers deemed it expedient....

This committee received evidence from Maj. Gen. Smedley D. Butler (retired), twice decorated by the Congress of the United States . . . your committee was able to verify all the pertinent statements made by General Butler....

John W. McCormack, Chairman, Special Committee on Un-American Activities, House of Representatives, February 15, 1935.

Just before Christmas 1934, news of a bizarre plot to install a dictator in the White House surfaced in Washington and New York, and the story—one of unparalled significance—was promptly smothered by Congress and the establishment press.[1]

On November 21, 1934 *The New York Times* printed the first portion of the Butler story as told to the House Un-American Activities Committee, giving it front-page treatment and an intriguing lead paragraph:

A plot of Wall Street interests to overthrow President Roosevelt and establish a fascist dictatorship, backed by a private army of 500,000 ex-

---

1. See Jules Archer, *The Plot to Seize the White House* (New York: Hawthorn Books, 1973) Archer's book is "the first effort to tell the whole story of the plot in sequence and full detail."

    Also see George Wolfskill, *The Revolt of the Conservatives* (Boston: Houghton,

soldiers and others, was charged by Major Gen. Smedley D. Butler, retired Marine Corps officer. . . .

The *New York Times* report added that General Butler, ". . . had told friends . . . that General Hugh S. Johnson, former NRA administrator, was scheduled for the role of dictator, and J.P. Morgan & Co. as well as Murphy & Co. were behind the plot."

After this promising opening, *The New York Times* reporting gradually faded away and finally disappeared. Fortunately, enough information has since surfaced to demonstrate that the Butler Affair or the Plot to Seize the White House is an integral part of our story of FDR and Wall Street.

GRAYSON M-P. MURPHY COMPANY, 52 BROADWAY

The central figure in the plot was Major General Smedley Darlington Butler, a colorful, popular, widely known Marine Corps officer, twice decorated with the Congressional Medal of Honor and a veteran of 33 years of military service. General Butler testified in 1934 to the McCormack-Dickstein Committee investigating Nazi and Communist activities in the United States that a plan for a White House dictatorship was outlined to him by two members of the American Legion: Gerald C. MacGuire, who worked for Grayson M-P. Murphy & Co., 52 Broadway, New York City, and Bill Doyle, whom Butler identified as an officer of the American Legion. General Butler testified that these men wanted to "unseat the Royal Family in control of the American Legion at the Convention to be held in Chicago, and [were] very anxious to have me take part in it." A scheme was outlined to General Butler: he was to come before the convention as a legion delegate from Honolulu; there would be two or three hundred American Legion members in the audience; and "these planted fellows were to begin to cheer and start a stampede and yell for a speech, then I was to go to the platform and make a speech."

Mifflin, 1962), which has extensive material on the plot. The interested reader should also take a look at George Seldes, *One Thousand Americans* (New York: Honi & Gaer, 1947).

Unfortunately, while these books have kept the event alive—a valiant effort that should by no means be underrated—they do reflect an amteurish confusion of fascism with moderation. Supporters of the Constitution would, of course, absolutely reject the dictatorial efforts described. Some groups, such as the American Conservative Union for instance, have for a decade aimed their attacks at the targets identified by Archer and Seldes. The misinterpretation by the latter authors is accentuated because confusion over the meaning of conservatism also prevented these authors from exploring the possibility that Wall Street had none other than Franklin Delano Roosevelt in mind as "the man on the white horse."

The prepared speech was to be written by Morgan associate John W. Davis. To prove his Wall Street financial backing, MacGuire showed General Butler a bank book listing deposits of $42,000 and $64,000 and mentioned that their source was Grayson M-P. Murphy, director of Guaranty Trust Company and other Morgan-controlled companies. A millionaire banker, Robert S. Clark, with offices in the Stock Exchange Building at 11 Wall Street, was also involved.

Robert Clark was incidentally known to General Butler from his China campaign days. MacGuire and Doyle also offered Butler a substantial sum to make a similar speech before the convention of the Veterans of Foreign Wars at Miami Beach. According to MacGuire, his group had investigated the background of Mussolini and Italian fascism, Hitler's organization in Germany, and the Croix de Feu in France and hinted that it was time to establish a similar organization in the United States. General Butler testified to the Congressional committee about MacGuire's statement in the following words:

> He said, "The time has come now to get the soldiers together."
> "Yes," I said, "I think so, too." He said, "I went abroad to study the part that the veteran plays in the various set-ups of the governments that they have abroad. I went to Italy for 2 or 3 months and studied the position that the veterans of Italy occupy in the Fascist set-up of Government, and I discovered that they are the background of Mussolini. They keep them on the pay rolls in various ways and keep them contented and happy; and they are his real backbone, the force on which he may depend, in case of trouble, to sustain him. But that set-up would not suit us at all. The soldiers of America would not like that. I then went to Germany to see what Hilter was doing, and his whole strength lies in organizations of soldiers, too. But that would not do. I looked into the Russian business. I found that the use of the soldiers over there would never appeal to our men. Then I went to France, and I found just exactly the organization we are going to have. It is an organization of supersoldiers." He gave me the French name for it, but I do not recall what it is. I never could have pronounced it, anyhow. But I do know that it is a superorganization of members of all the other soldiers' organizations of France, composed of noncommissioned officers and officers. He told me that they had about 500,000 and that each one was a leader of 10 others, so that it gave them 5,000,000 votes. And he said, "Now, that is our idea here in America—to get up an organization of that kind."[2]

What would be the objective of this superorganization? According to the previously cited *New York Times*,[3] General Butler is reported to have testified that the affair was an attempted *coup d'état* to overthrow President Roosevelt and replace him with a fascist dictator. This inter-

2. House of Representatives, *Investigation of Nazi Propaganda Activities and Investigation of Certain Other Propaganda Activities*, Hearings No. 73-D.C.-6, op. cit., p. 17.
3. *The New York Times*, Nov. 21, 1934.

pretation is repeated by Archer, Seldes, and other writers. However, this was *not* the accusation made by General Butler to the committee. Butler's precise statement concerning the projected organization, the use to which it was to be put when established, and the role of President Roosevelt is as follows; General Butler reported on his conversation with MacGuire:

I said, "What do you want to do with it when you get it up?"

"Well," he said, "we want to support the President."

I said, "The President does not need the support of that kind of an organization. Since when did you become a supporter of the President? The last time I talked to you you were against him."

He said, "Well, he is going to go along with us now."

"Is he?"

"Yes."

"Well, what are you going to do with these men, suppose you get these 500,000 men in America? What are you going to do with them?"

"Well," he said, "they will be the support of the President."

I said, "The President has got the whole American people. Why does he want them?"

He said, "Don't you understand the set-up has got to be changed a bit? Now, we have got him—we have got the President. He has got to have more money. There is not any more money to give him. Eighty percent of the money now is in Government bonds, and he cannot keep this racket up much longer. He has got to do something about it. He has either got to get more money out of us or he has got to change the method of financing the Government, and we are going to see to it that he does not change that method. He will not change it."

I said, "The idea of this great group of soldiers, then, is to sort of frighten him, is it?"

"No, no, no; not to frighten him. This is to sustain him when others assault him."

I said, "Well I do not know about that. How would the President explain it?"

He said: "He will not necessarily have to explain it, because we are going to help him out. Now, did it ever occur to you that the President is overworked? We might have an Assistant President, somebody to take the blame; and if things do not work out, he can drop him."

He went on to say that it did not take any constitutional change to authorize another Cabinet official, somebody to take over the details of the office—take them off the President's shoulders. He mentioned that the position would be a secretary of general affairs—a sort of supersecretary.

CHAIRMAN [Congressman McCormack]. A secretary of general affairs?

BUTLER. That is the term used by him—or a secretary of general welfare—I cannot recall which. I came out of the interview with that name in my head. I got that idea from talking to both of them, you see. They had both talked about the same kind of relief that ought to be given the President, and he said: "You know, the American people will swallow that. We have got the newspapers. We will start a campaign that the President's health is failing. Everybody can tell that by looking at him,

146

and the dumb American people will fall for it in a second." And I could see it. They had that sympathy racket, that they were going to have somebody take the patronage off of his shoulders and take all the worries and details off of his shoulders, and then he will be like the President of France. I said, "So that is where you got this idea?"

He said: "I have been traveling around looking around. Now, about this superorganization—would you be interested in heading it?"

I said, "I am interested in it, but I do not know about heading it. I am very greatly interested in it, because you know, Jerry, my interest is, my one hobby is, maintaining a democracy. If you get these 500,000 soldiers advocating anything smelling of Fascism, I am going to get 500,000 more and lick the hell out of you, and we will have a real war right at home. You know that."

"Oh, no. We do not want that. We want to ease up on the President."

"Yes; and then you will put somebody in there you can run; is that the idea? The President will go around and christen babies and dedicate bridges, and kiss children. Mr. Roosevelt will never agree to that himself."

"Oh yes; he will. He will agree to that."[4]

In other words, the Wall Street plot was not to dispose of President Roosevelt at all, but to kick him upstairs and install an Assistant President with absolute powers. Just why it was necessary to go to the trouble of installing an Assistant President is unclear because the Vice President was in office. In any event, it was planned to run the United States with a Secretary of General Affairs, and the gullible American public would accept this under the guise of necessary protection from a communist take-over.

At this point it is interesting to recall the role of many of these same financiers and financial firms in the Bolshevik Revolution—a role, incidentally, that could *not* have been known to General Butler[5]—and the use of similar Red scare tactics in the 1922 United Americans organization. Grayson M-P. Murphy was, in the early 1930s, a director of several companies controlled by the J.P. Morgan interests, including the Guaranty Trust Company, prominent in the Bolshevik Revolution, the New York Trust Company, and Bethlehem Steel, and was on the board of Inspiration Copper Company, National Aviation Corporation, Intercontinental Rubber Co., and U.S. & Foreign Securities. John W. Davis, the speech writer for General Butler, was a partner in Davis, Polk, Wardwell, Gardner & Reed of 15 Broad Street. Both Polk and Wardwell of this prestigious law firm, as well as Grayson Murphy, had roles in the Bolshevik Revolution. Further, Davis was also a codirector with

4. House of Representatives, *Investigation of Nazi Propaganda Activities and Investigation of Certain Other Propaganda Activities,* Hearings No. 73-D.C.-6, op. cit., pp. 17-18.

5. See Sutton, *Bolshevik Revolution,* op. cit.

Murphy in the Morgan-controlled Guaranty Trust Co. and a codirector with Presidential hopeful Al Smith in the Metropolitan Life Insurance Co., as well as director of the Mutual Life Insurance Co., the U.S. Rubber Co., and American Telephone and Telegraph, the controlling unit of the Bell System.

Fortunately for history, General Butler discussed the offer with an impartial newspaper source at a very early point in his talks with MacGuire and Doyle. The McCormack-Dickstein Committee heard testimony under oath from this confidant, Paul Comley French. French confirmed the facts that he was a reporter for *The Philadelphia Record* and the *The New York Evening Post* and that General Butler had told him about the plot in September 1934. Subsequently, on September 13, 1934 French went to New York and met with MacGuire. The following is part of French's statement to the Committee:

MR. FRENCH. [I saw] Gerald P. MacGuire in the offices of Grayson M.-P. Murphy & Co., the twelfth floor of 52 Broadway, shortly after 1 o'clock in the afternoon. He has a small private office there and I went into his office. I have here some direct quotes from him. As soon as I left his office I got to a typewriter and made a memorandum of everything that he told me. "We need a Fascist government in this country," he insisted, "to save the Nation from the communists who want to tear it down and wreck all that we have built in America. The only men who have the patriotism to do it are the soldiers and Smedley Butler is the ideal leader. He could organize a million men over night." During the conversation he told me he had been in Italy and Germany during the summer of 1934 and the spring of 1934 and had made an intensive study of the background of the Nazi and Fascist movements and how the veterans had played a part in them. He said he had obtained enough information on the Fascist and Nazi movements and of the part played by the veterans, to properly set up one in this country.

He emphasized throughout his conversation with me that the whole thing was tremendously patriotic, that it was saving the Nation from communists, and that the men they deal with have that crackbrained idea that the Communists are going to take it apart. He said the only safeguard would be the soldiers. At first he suggested that the General organize this outfit himself and ask a dollar a year dues from everybody. We discussed that, and then he came around to the point of getting outside financial funds, and he said that it would not be any trouble to raise a million dollars.

During the course of the conversation he continually discussed the need of a man on a white horse, as he called it, a dictator who would come galloping in on his white horse. He said that was the only way; either through the threat of armed force or the delegation of power, and the use of a group of organized veterans, to save the capitalistic system.

He warmed up considerably after we got under way and he said, "We might go along with Roosevelt, and then do with him what Mussolini did with the King of Italy." It fits in with what he told the general [Butler], that we would have a Secretary of General Affairs, and if Roosevelt played ball, swell; and if he did not, they would push him out.[6]

JACKSON MARTINDELL, 14 WALL STREET

The sworn testimony of General Smedley Butler and Paul French in the committee hearings has a persistent thread. General Butler rambled from time to time, and some parts of his statement are vague, but there is obviously a lot more to the story than an innocent gathering of American Legion members into a superorganization. Is there any independent evidence to confirm General Butler and Paul French? Unknown to both Butler and French, Guaranty Trust had been involved in Wall Street maneuverings in the Bolshevik Revolution in 1917, so indicating at least a predisposition to mix financial business with dictatorial politics; two of the persons involved in the plot were directors of Guaranty Trust. Also, before the hearings were abruptly halted, the committee heard evidence from an independent source, which confirmed many details recounted by General Butler and Paul French. In December 1934 Captain Samuel Glazier, Commanding Officer of the CCC Camp at Elkridge, Maryland,[7] was called before the committee.

On October 2, 1934, testified Captain Glazier, he had received a letter from A.P. Sullivan, Assistant Adjutant General of the U.S. Army, introducing a Mr. Jackson Martindell, "who will be shown every courtesy by you." This letter was sent to Glazier by command of Major General Malone of the U.S. Army. Who was Jackson Martindell? He was a financial counsel with offices at 14 Wall Street, previously associated with Stone & Webster & Blodget, Inc., investment bankers of 120 Broadway, and with Carter, Martindell & Co., investment bankers at 115 Broadway.[8] Martindell was a man of substance, living according to *The New York Times*, ". . . in the centre of a beautiful sixty acre estate" that he had bought from Charles Pfizer,[9] and was sufficiently influential for General Malone to arrange a conducted tour of the Elkridge, Maryland Conservation Corps Camp.

Martindell's association with Stone & Webster (120 Broadway) is

6. House of Representatives, *Investigation of Nazi Propaganda Activities and Investigation of Certain Other Propaganda Activities*, Hearings No. 73-D.C.-6, op. cit., p. 26.

7. Ibid., Parts 1-2. Based on Testimony before the McCormack-Dickstein Committee.

8. 120 Broadway is the topic of a chapter in this book and a previous book, Sutton, *Bolshevik Revolution*, op. cit. Stone & Webster is also prominent in the earlier book.

9. *The New York Times*, Dec. 28, 1934.

significant and by itself warrants a follow-up on his associates in the Wall Street area.

Captain Glazier provided Martindell with the requested camp tour and testified to the committee that Martindell posed numerous questions about a similar camp for men to work in industry rather than in forests. A week or so after the visit, Captain Glazier visited Martindell's New Jersey home, learned that he was a personal friend of General Malone, and was informed that Martindell wanted to organize camps similar to the CCC to train 500,000 young men. The overtones of this talk, as reported by Glazier, were anti-semitic and suggested an attempted *coup d'etat* in the United States; the organization sponsoring this overthrow was called American Vigilantes, whose emblem was a flag with a red eagle on a blue background in lieu of the German swastika. This was in part an independent verification of General Butler's testimony.

GERALD C. MACGUIRE'S TESTIMONY

Gerald MacGuire, one of the accused plotters, was called before the committee and testified at length under oath. He stated that he met General Butler in 1933 and that his reasons for visiting Butler were, (1) to discuss the Committee for a Sound Dollar and (2) that he thought Butler would be a "fine man to be commander of the Legion."

MacGuire admitted that he had told General Butler that he was a member of the distinguished guest committee of the American Legion; he had a "hazy recollection" that millionaire Robert S. Clark had talked to Butler, but "denied emphatically" making arrangements for Clark to meet Butler. MacGuire admitted sending Butler postcards from Europe, that he had had a conversation with the general at the Bellevue-Stratford Hotel, and that he had told Butler that he was going to the convention in Miami. However, when asked whether he had told Butler about the role veterans played in European governments, he replied that he had not, although he stated that he had told Butler that in his opinion "Hitler would not last another year in Germany and that Mussolini was on the skids."[10]

MacGuire's testimony on his meeting with French differed substantially from French's account:

QUESTION. Now, what did Mr. French call to see you about, Mr. MacGuire?

ANSWER. He called, according to Mr. French's story, to meet me, and to make my acquaintance, because I had known General Butler, and I

10. House of Representatives, *Investigation of Nazi Propaganda Activities and Investigation of Certain Other Propaganda Activities,* Hearings No. 73-D.C.-6, op. cit., p. 45.

was a friend of his, and he wanted to know me, and that was mainly the object of his visit.

QUESTION. Nothing else discussed?

ANSWER. A number of things discussed; yes. The position of the bond market, the stock market; what I thought was a good buy right now; what he could buy if he had seven or eight hundred dollars; the position of the country; the prospects for recovery, and various topics that any two men would discuss if they came together.

QUESTION. Nothing else?

ANSWER. Nothing else, excepting this, Mr. Chairman: As I said yesterday, I believe, when Mr. French came to me, he said, General Butler is, or has, again been approached by two or three organizations—and I think he mentioned one of them as some Vigilante committee of this country— and he said, "What do you think of it?" and I think I said to him, "Why, I don't think the General ought to get mixed up with any of those affairs in this country. I think these fellows are all trying to use him; to use his name for publicity purposes, and to get membership, and I think he ought to keep away from any of these organizations."

QUESTION. Nothing else?

ANSWER. Nothing else. That was the gist of the entire conversation.[11]

MacGuire further testified that he worked for Grayson Murphy and that Robert S. Clark had put up $300,000 to form the Committee for a Sound Dollar.

The McCormack-Dickstein Committee was able to confirm the fact that Robert Sterling Clark transmitted money to MacGuire for political purposes:

He [MacGuire] further testified that this money was given him by Mr. Clark long after the Chicago Convention of the Legion, and that he had also received from Walter E. Frew of the Corn Exchange Bank & Trust Co. the sum of $1,000, which was also placed to the credit of the Sound Money Committee.

MacGuire then testified that he had received from Robert Sterling Clark approximately $7200, for his traveling expenses to, in and from Europe, to which had been added the sum of $2500 on another occasion and $1000 at another time, and he stated under oath, that he had not received anything from anybody else and further testified that he had deposited it in his personal account at the Manufacturers Trust Co., 55 Broad Street.

MacGuire further testified that he had a drawing account of $432 a month right now, to which were added some commissions. Later MacGuire testified that the $2500 and the $1000 were in connection with the organization of the Committee for a Sound Dollar.

Chairman McCormack then directed the following question: "Did Mr. Clark contribute any money in any other way, besides the $30,000. and the other sums that you have enumerated he gave to you personally?" to which MacGuire replied, "No sir, he has been asked several times to contribute to different funds, but he has refused."[12]

11. Ibid., p. 45.
12. Press release, New York City, p. 12.

In its New York press release the committee noted several discrepancies in MacGuire's testimony on receipt of funds. The section reads as follows:

> Neither could MacGuire remember what the purpose of his trip was to Washington or whether he had given the Central Hanover Bank thirteen one thousand dollar bills or that he had bought one of the letters of credit with a certified check drawn on the account of Mr. Christmas.
>
> In the course of the questioning MacGuire could not remember whether he had ever handled thousand dollar bills, and certainly could not remember producing thirteen of them at one time in the bank. It must be remembered in this connection, that the $13,000 purchase with one thousand dollar bills at the bank, came just six days after Butler claims MacGuire showed him eighteen one thousand dollars bills in Newark.
>
> From the foregoing, it can readily be seen that in addition to the $30,000 which Clark gave MacGuire for the Sound Money Committee that he produced approximately $75,000 more which MacGuire reluctantly admitted on being confronted with the evidence.
>
> This $75,000 is shown in the $26,000 that went into the Manufacturers Trust account, $10,000 in currency at the luncheon, the purchase of letters of credit toaling $30,300, of which Christmas' certified check was represented as $15,000, expenses to Europe close to $8,000. This still stands unexplained.
>
> Whether there was more and how much, the Committee does not yet know.[13]

The committee then asked MacGuire an obvious question: whether he knew Jackson Martindell. Unfortunately, an equally obvious error in MacGuire's answer was allowed to pass by unchallenged. The committee transcript reads as follows:

> *By the Chairman:*
> QUESTION. Do you know Mr. Martindell, Mr. MacGuire?
> ANSWER. Mr. Martin Dell? No, sir; I do not.
> THE CHAIRMAN. Is that his name?
> MR. DICKSTEIN. I think so.[14]

So, in brief, we have three reliable witnesses—General Butler, Paul French, and Captain Samuel Glazier—testifying under oath about plans of a plot to install a dictatorship in the United States. And we have contradictory testimony from Gerald MacGuire that clearly warrants further investigation. Such investigation was at first the committee's stated intention: "The Committee is awaiting the return to this country of both Mr. Clark and Mr. Christmas. As the evidence stands,

13. Ibid., p. 13.
14. House of Representatives, *Investigation of Nazi Propaganda Activities and Investigation of Certain Other Propaganda Activities,* Hearings No. 73-D.C.-6, op. cit., p. 85.

it calls for an explanation that the Committee has been unable to obtain from Mr. MacGuire."[15]

But the Committee did *not* call either Mr. Clark or Mr. Christmas to give evidence. It made no further effort—at least, no further effort appears on the public record—to find an explanation for the inconsistencies and inaccuracies in MacGuire's testimony, testimony that was given to the committee under oath.

SUPPRESSION OF WALL STREET INVOLVEMENT

The story of an attempted take-over of executive power in the United States was suppressed, not only by parties directly interested, but also by several institutions usually regarded as protectors of constitutional liberty and freedom of inquiry. Among the groups suppressing information were (1) the Congress of the United States, (2) the press, notably *Time* and *The New York Times*, and (3) the White House itself. It is also notable that no academic inquiry has been conducted into what is surely one of the more ominous events in recent American history. Suppression is even more regrettable in the light of the current trend toward collectivism in the United States and the likelihood of another attempt at a dictatorial takeover using supposed threats from either the left or the right as a pretext.

Suppression by the House Un-American Activities Committee took the form of deleting extensive excerpts relating to Wall Street financiers including Guaranty Trust director Grayson Murphy, J.P. Morgan, the Du Pont interests, Remington Arms, and others allegedly involved in the plot attempt. Even today, in 1975, a full transcript of the hearings cannot be traced.

Some of the deleted portions of the transcript were unearthed by reporter John Spivak.[16] A reference to NRA Administrator Hugh Johnson will show the type of information suppressed; the Committee suppressed the words in italics from the printed testimony; Butler speaks to MacGuire:

> I said, "Is there anthing stirring about it yet?"
> "Yes," he says; "you watch; in two or three weeks you will see it come out in the papers. There will be big fellows in it" . . .*and in about two weeks the American Liberty League appeared, which was just about what he described it to be.*

15. Press release, New York City, p. 13.
16. See Jules Archer, *The Plot to Seize the White House,* op. cit.

We might have an assistant President, somebody to take the blame; and if things do not work out, he can drop him. *He said, "That is what he was building up Hugh Johnson for. Hugh Johnson talked too damn much and got him into a hole, and he is going to fire him in the next three or four weeks."*

I said, "How do you know all this?" "Oh," he said, "we are in with him all the time. We know what is going to happen."[17]

The testimony of Paul French was also censored by the House Committee. Witness the following extract from French's testimony referring to John W. Davis, J.P. Morgan, the Du Pont Company, and others in Wall Street and which strongly corroborates General Butler's testimony:

At first he [MacGuire] suggested that the General [Butler] organize this outfit himself and ask a dollar a year dues from everybody. We discussed that, and then he came around to the point of getting outside financial funds, and he said it would not be any trouble to raise a million dollars. *He said he could go to John W. Davis [attorney for J.P. Morgan & Co.] or Perkins of the National City Bank, and any number of persons to get it. Of course, that may or may not mean anything. That is, his reference to John W. Davis and Perkins of the National City Bank. During my conversation with him I did not of course commit the General to anything. I was just feeling him along. Later, we discussed the question of arms and equipment, and he suggested that they could be obtained from the Remington Arms Co., on credit through the Du Ponts.*

I do not think at that time he mentioned the connections of Du Pont with the American Liberty League, but he skirted all around it. That is, I do not think he mentioned the Liberty League, but he skirted all around the idea that that was the back door; one of the Du Ponts is on the board of directors of the American Liberty League and they own a controlling interest in the Remington Arms Co . . . He said the General would not have any trouble enlisting 500,000 men.[18]

John L. Spivak, the reporter who unearthed the suppression in the Congressional transcripts, challenged Committee Cochairman Samuel Dickstein of New York with his evidence. Dickstein admitted that:

the Committee had deleted certain parts of the testimony because they were hearsay."

"But your published reports are full of hearsay testimony."

"They are?" he said.

"Why wasn't Grayson Murphy called? Your Committee knew that Murphy's men are in the anti-Semetic espionage organization Order of '76?"

"We didn't have the time. We'd have taken care of the Wall Street groups if we had the time. I would have no hesitation in going after the Morgans."

17. George Seldes, *One Thousand Americans*, op. cit., p. 288.
18. Ibid., pp. 289-290.

"You had Belgrano, Commander of the American Legion, listed to testify. Why wasn't he examined?"

"I don't know. Maybe you can get Mr. McCormack to explain that. I had nothing to do with it."[19]

The fact remains that the committee did not call Grayson Murphy, Jackson Martindell, or John W. Davis, all directly accused in sworn testimony. Further, the committee deleted all portions of the testimony involving other prominent persons: J.P. Morgan, the Du Ponts, the Rockefeller interests, Hugh Johnson, and Franklin D. Roosevelt. When Congressman Dickstein pleaded his innocence to John Spivak, it was inconsistent with his own letter to President Roosevelt, in which he claims to have placed restrictions even upon public distribution of the committee hearings, as printed, "in order that they might not get into other than responsible hands." The final report issued by the committee in February 15, 1935 buried the story even further. John L. Spivak sums up the burial succinctly: "I . . . studied the Committee's report. It gave six pages to the threat by Nazi agents operating in this country and eleven pages to the threat by communists. It gave one page to the plot to seize the Government and destroy our democratic system."[20]

The role of leading newspapers and journals of opinion in reporting the Butler affair is equally suspect. In fact, their handling of the event has the appearance of outright distortion and censorship. The veracity of some major newspapers has been widely questioned in the last 50 years,[21] and in some quarters the media have even been accused of a conspiracy to suppress "everything in opposition to the wishes of the interest served." For example, in 1917 Congressman Callaway inserted in *The Congressional Record* the following devastating critique of Morgan control of the press:

MR. CALLAWAY. Mr. Chairman, under unanimous consent, I insert in the *Record* at this point a statement showing the newspaper combination, which explains their activity in this war matter, just discussed by the gentleman from Pennsylvania (Mr. Moore):

In March, 1915, the J.P. Morgan interests, the steel, shipbuilding, and powder interests, and their subsidiary organizations, got together 12 men high up in the newspaper world and employed them to select the most influential newspapers in the United States and a sufficient number of them to control generally the policy of the daily press of the United States.

These 12 men worked the problem out by selecting 179 newspapers,

---

19. John L. Spivak, *A Man in his Time* (New York: Horizon Press, 1967), pp. 311, 322-25.

20. Ibid., p. 331.

21. See Herman Dinsmore, *All the News That Fits,* (New Rochelle: Arlington House, 1969).

155

and then began by an elimination process, to retain only those necessary for the purpose of controlling the general policy of the daily press throughout the country. They found it was only necessary to purchase the control of 25 of the greatest papers. The 25 papers were agreed upon; emissaries were sent to purchase the policy, national and international, of these papers; an agreement was reached; the policy of the papers was bought, to be paid for by the month; an editor was furnished for each paper to properly supervise and edit information regarding the questions of preparedness, militarism, financial policies, and other things of national and international nature considered vital to the interests of the purchasers.

This contract is in existence at the present time, and it accounts for the news columns of the daily press of the country being filled with all sorts of preparedness arguments and misrepresentations as to the present condition of the United States Army and Navy and the possibility and probability of the United States being attacked by foreign foes.

This policy also included the suppression of everything in opposition to the wishes of the interests served. The effectiveness of this scheme has been conclusively demonstrated by the character of stuff carried in the daily press throughout the country since March 1915. They have resorted to anything necessary to commercialize public sentiment and sandbag the National Congress into making extravagant and wasteful appropriations for the Army and Navy under the false pretense that it was necessary. Their stock argument is that it is "patriotism." They are playing on every prejudice and passion of the American people.[22]

In the Butler affair the accused interests are also those identified by Congressman Callaway: the J.P. Morgan firm and the steel and powder industries. General Butler accused Grayson Murphy, a director of the Morgan-controlled Guaranty Trust Company; Jackson Martindell, associated with Stone & Webster, allied to the Morgans; the Du Pont Company (the powder industry); and Remington Arms Company, which was controlled by Du Pont and the Morgan-Harriman financial interests. Further, the firms that appear in the suppressed 1934 Congressional testimony are J.P. Morgan, Du Pont, and Remington Arms. In brief, we can verify 1934 Congressional suppression of information that supports the earlier 1917 charges of Congressman Callaway.

Does such suppression extend to major news journals? We can take two prime examples: *The New York Times* and *Time* magazine. If such a combination as Callaway charges did exist, then these two journals would certainly be among "25 of the greatest papers involved in the 1930s." *The New York Times* reporting of the "plot" opens up with a front-page headline article on November 21, 1934: "Gen. Butler Bares 'Fascist Plot' to Seize Government by Force," with the lead paragraph quoted above (p. 143). This *Times* article is a reasonably good job of reporting and includes a forthright statement by Congressman Dick-

---

22. *Congressional Record*, Vol. 55, pp. 2947-8 (1917).

stein: "From present indications Butler has the evidence. He's not going to make any serious charges unless he has something to back them up. We'll have men here with bigger names than his." Then the *Times* article records that "Mr. Dickstein said that about sixteen persons mentioned by General Butler to the Committee would be subpoenaed, and that a public hearing might be held next Monday." The *Times* also includes outright and sometimes enraged denials from Hugh Johnson, Thomas W. Lamont, and Grayson M–P. Murphy of Guaranty Trust.

The following morning, November 22, the *Times* made a major switch in reporting the plot. The disclosures were removed to an inside page, although the testimony now concerned Gerald MacGuire, one of the accused plotters. Further, a decided change in the attitude of the committee can be discerned. Congressman McCormack is now reported as saying that "the committee has not decided whether to call any additional witnesses. He said that the most important witness, aside from Mr. MacGuire, was Robert Sterling Clark, a wealthy New Yorker with offices in the Stock Exchange Building."

While the *Times* reporting was consigned to an inside single column, the editorial page, its most influential section, carried a lead editorial that set the tone for subsequent reporting. Under the head "Credulity Unlimited," it contended that the Butler charge was a "bald and unconvincing narrative. . . . The whole story sounds like a gigantic hoax . . . it does not merit serious discussion," and so on. In brief, *before* the 16 important witnesses were called, *before* the evidence was on the record, *before* the charge was investigated, *The New York Times* decided that it wanted to hear nothing about *this* story because it was a hoax, not fit to print.

The next day, November 23, the *Times* changed its reporting still further. The headlines were now about Reds and Red Union Strife and concerned alleged activities by communists in American trade unions, while the Butler testimony and the developing evidence were secreted deep within the reporting of Red activities. The resulting story was, of course, vague and confused, but it effectively buried the Butler evidence.

On November 26, the hearings continued, but the committee itself now had cold feet and issued a statement: "This Committee has had no evidence before it that would in the slightest degree warrant calling before it such men as John W. Davis, General Hugh Johnson, General James G. Harbord, Thomas W. Lamont, Admiral William S. Sims, or Hanford MacNider."

It should be noted that these names had come up in sworn testimony, later to be deleted from the official record. The *Times* pursued its reporting of this development in abbreviated form on an inside page under the head, "Committee Calm over Butler 'Plot', Has No Evidence to Warrant Calling Johnson and Others." On November 27 the *Times* reporting declined to five column inches on an inside page under the ominous head "Butler Plot Inquiry Not To Be Dropped." The December hearings were reported by the *Times* on a front page (December 28 1934), but the plot was now twisted to "Reds Plot to Kidnap the President, Witness Charges at House Inquiry."

Reviewing the story of the Butler Affair in the *Times* 40 years after the event and comparing its story to the printed official testimony, itself heavily censored, it is obvious that the newspaper, either under its own intiative or under outside pressure, decided that the story was not to be made public. Consistent with this interpretation, we find that *The New York Times*, the "newspaper of record," omits the Butler testimony from entries in its annual index, depended upon by researchers and scholars. The *Times Index* for 1934 has an entry "BUTLER (Maj Gen), Smedley D," but lists only a few of his speeches and a biographic portrait. The Butler testimony is not listed. There is an entry, "See also: Fascism-U.S.," but under that cross-reference there is listed only: "Maj Gen S.D. Butler charges plot to overthrow present govt; Wall Street interests and G.P. MacGuire implicated at Cong com hearing." The only significant Wall Street name mentioned in the index is that of R.S. Clark, who is reported as "puzzled" by the charges. None of the key Morgan and Du Pont associates cited by General Butler is listed in the *Index*. In other words, there appears to have been a deliberate attempt by this newspaper to mislead historians.

Time magazine's reporting descended to fiction in its attempts to reduce General Butler's evidence to the status of absurdity. If ever a student wants to construct an example of biased reporting, there is a first-rate example in a comparison of the evidence presented to the McCormack-Dickstein Committee by General Butler with the subsequent *Time* reportage. The December 3rd 1934 issue of *Time* ran the story under the head "Plot Without Plotters," but the story bears no resemblance at all to the testimony, not even the censored testimony. The story portrays General Butler leading a half-million men along U.S. Highway 1 with the cry, "Men, Washington is but 30 miles away! Will you follow me?" Butler was then depicted as taking over the U.S. government by force from President Roosevelt. The remainder of the *Time* story is filled with dredges from Butler's past and an assortment of denials from the accused. Nowhere is there any attempt to report the statements made by General Butler, although the denials by J.P. Morgan, Hugh Johnson, Robert Sterling Clark, and Grayson Murphy are cited correctly. Two photographs are included: a genial grandfatherly J.P. Morgan and General Butler in a pose that universally symbolizes lunacy—a finger pointed to his ear. The reporting was trashy, dishonest, and disgraceful journalism at its very worst. Whatever our thoughts may be on Nazi propaganda or Soviet press distortion, neither Goebbels nor *Goslit* ever attained the hypnotic expertise of *Time's* journalists and editors. The fearful problem is that the opinions and mores of millions of Americans and of English speakers around the world have been molded by this school of distorted journalism.

To keep our criticism in perspective, it must be noted that *Time* was apparently impartial in its pursuit of lurid journalism. Even Hugh S. Johnson, administrator of NRA and one of the alleged plotters in the Butler Affair, was a target of *Time's* mischief. As Johnson reports it in his book:

> I stood in the reviewing stand in that parade and there were hundreds of people I knew who waved as they went past. Down below were massed batteries of cameras, and I knew if I raised my hand higher than my shoulders, it would seem and be publicized as a "Fascist salute." So I never did raise it higher. I just stuck my arm out straight and wiggled my hand around. But that didn't help me—*Time* came out saying I had constantly saluted *au Mussolini* and even had a photograph to prove it, *but it wasn't my arm* on that photograph. It wore the taped cuff sleeve of a cut-away coat and a stiff round cuff with an old fashioned cuff button and I never wore either in my whole life. I think it was the arm of Mayor O'Brien who stood beside me which had been faked onto my body.[23]

AN ASSESSMENT OF THE BUTLER AFFAIR

The most important point to be assessed is the credibility of General Smedley Darlington Butler. Was General Butler lying? Was he telling the truth? Was he exaggerating for the sake of effect?

General Butler was an unusual man and a particularly unusual man to find in the armed forces: decorated twice with the Medal of Honor, an unquestioned leader of men, with undoubted personal bravery, deep loyalty to his fellow men, and a fierce sense of justice. All these are admirable qualities. Certainly, General Butler was hardly the type of man to tell lies or even exaggerate for a petty reason. His flair for the dramatic does leave open a possibility of exaggeration, but deliberate lying is most unlikely.

Does the evidence support or reject Butler? Reporter Paul French of *The Philadelphia Record* wholly supports Butler. Evidence by Captain Glazier, commander of the CCC camp, supports Butler. In these two

23. Hugh S. Johnson, *The Blue Eagle from Egg to Earth,* op. cit., p. 267.

cases there is no discrepancy in the evidence. The statements of MacGuire made under oath to Congress do not support Butler. We have therefore a conflict of sworn evidence. Further, MacGuire was found at fault on several points by the committee; he used the evasion of "do not recall" on a number of occasions and, in major areas such as the financing by Clark, MacGuire unwillingly supports Butler. There is a hard core of plausibility to the Butler story. There is some possibility of exaggeration, perhaps not untypical for a man of Butler's flamboyant personality, but this is neither proven nor disproven.

Without question, the Congress of the United States did a grave disservice to the cause of freedom in suppressing the Butler story. Let us hope that some Congressmen or some Congressional committee, even at this late date, will pick up the threads and release the full uncensored testimony. We may also hope that the next time around, in some comparably important matter, *The New York Times* will live up to its claim to be the newspaper of record, a name it justified so admirably four decades later in the Watergate Investigation.

CHAPTER 11

The Corporate Socialists
at 120 Broadway, New York City

> Already he [FDR] had begun to reappear at the office of the Fidelity and
> Deposit Company at 120 Broadway. He did not yet visit his law office at
> 52 Wall Street, because of the high front steps—he could not bear the
> thought of being carried up them in public. At 120 Broadway he could
> manage, by himself, the one little step up from the sidewalk.
> *Frank Freidel,* Franklin D. Roosevelt: The Ordeal (*Boston: Little,
> Brown, 1954), p. 119.*

As in *Wall Street and the Bolshevik Revolution,* we find many of the
leading characters (including FDR) and firms, even a few of the events,
described in this book located at a single address, the Equitable Office
Building at 120 Broadway, New York City.

Franklin D. Roosevelt's office in the early 1920s when he was vice
president of the Fidelity and Deposit Company was at 120 Broadway.
Biographer Frank Freidel records above his reentry to the building
after his crippling polio attack. At that time, Bernard Baruch's office
was also at 120 Broadway and Hugh Johnson, later to be the administrator of NRA, was Bernard Baruch's research assistant at the same
address. The executive offices of General Electric and the offices of
Gerard Swope, author of the Swope Plan that became Roosevelt's
NRA, were also there. The Bankers Club was on the top floor of this

same Equitable Office Building and was the location of a 1926 meeting by the Butler Affair plotters. Obviously, there was a concentration of talent at this particular address deserving greater description.

THE BOLSHEVIK REVOLUTION AND 120 BROADWAY

In *Wall Street and the Bolshevik Revolution,* we noted that revolution-related financiers were concentrated at a single address in New York City, the same Equitable Office Building. In 1917 the headquarters of the No. 2 District of the Federal Reserve System, the most important of the Federal Reserve districts, was located at 120 Broadway; of nine directors of the Federal Reserve Bank of New York, four were physically located at 120 Broadway, and two of these directors were simultaneously on the board of American International Corporation. The American International Corporation had been founded in 1915 by the Morgan interests with enthusiastic participation by the Rockefeller and Stillman groups. The general offices of A.I.C. were at 120 Broadway. Its directors were heavily interlocked with other major Wall Street financial and industrial interests, and it was determined that American International Corporation had a significant role in the success and consolidation of the 1917 Bolshevik Revolution. A.I.C. executive secretary William Franklin Sands, asked for his opinion of the Bolshevik Revolution by the State Department within a few weeks of the outbreak in November 1917 (long before even a fraction of Russia came under Soviet control), expressed strong support for the revolution. Sands' letter is reprinted in *Wall Street and the Bolshevik Revolution.* A memorandum to David Lloyd George, Prime Minister of England, from Morgan associate Dwight Morrow also urged support for the Bolshevik revolutionaries and backing for its armies. A director of the FRB of New York, William Boyce Thompson, donated $1 million to the Bolshevik cause and intervened with Lloyd George on behalf of the emerging Soviets.

In brief, we found an identifiable pattern of pro-Bolshevik activity by influential members of Wall Street concentrated in the Federal Reserve Bank of New York and the American International Corporation, both at 120 Broadway. By 1933 the bank had moved to Liberty Street.

THE FEDERAL RESERVE BANK OF NEW YORK AND 120 BROADWAY

The names of individual FRB directors changed between 1917 and the 1930s, but it was determined that, although the FRB had moved, four

162

FRB directors still had offices at this address in the New Deal period, as shown in the following table:

Directors of the Federal Reserve Bank of New York in the New Deal Period

Name	Directorships Held for Companies Located at 120 Broadway
Charles E. Mitchell	Director of the FRB of New York, 1929-1931, and director of Corporation Trust Co. (120 Broadway)
Albert H. Wiggin	Succeeded Charles E. Mitchell as Director, FRB of New York, 1932-34, and Director of American International Corp, and Stone and Webster, Inc. (both 120 Broadway)
Clarence M. Woolley	Director FRB of New York, 1922-1936, and director, General Electric Co. (120 Broadway)
Owen D. Young	Director FRB of New York, 1927-1935, and chairman, General Electric Co. (120 Broadway)

Persons and firms located at:

120 BROADWAY

Franklin Delano Roosevelt
Bernard Baruch
Gerard Swope
Owen D. Young

42 BROADWAY

Herbert Clark Hoover

OTHERS:

American International Corp.
The Corporation Trust Co.
Empire Trust Co.
Fidelity Trust Co.
American Smelting & Refining Co.
Armour & Co. (New York Office).
Baldwin Locomotive Works
Federal Mining & Smelting Co.
General Electric Co.
Kennecott Copper Corp.
Metal & Thermit Corp.
National Dairy Products Corp.
Yukon Gold Co.
Stone & Webster & Blodget, Inc.

Grayson M–P Murphy (52 Broadway)
International Acceptance Bank, Inc. (52 Cedar St.)
International Acceptance Trust Co. (52 Cedar St.)
International Manhattan Co. Inc. (52 Cedar St.)
Jackson Martindell (14 Wall St.)
John D. Rockefeller, Jr. (26 Broadway)
Percy A. Rockefeller (25 Broadway)
Robert S. Clark (11 Wall St.)

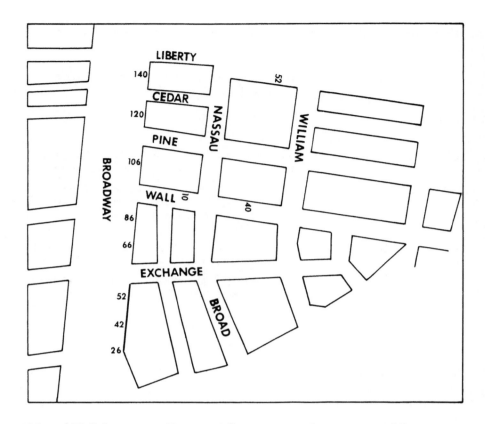

Map of Wall Street Area Showing Office Locations for persons and firms mentioned in this book.

AMERICAN INTERNATIONAL CORPORATION
AND 120 BROADWAY

The American International Corporation (AIC) was formed in 1915 by a coalition of Morgan, Stillman and Rockefeller interests; its general offices were at 120 Braodway from 1915 through the 1920s. The great excitement in Wall Street about formation of AIC brought about a concentration of the most powerful financial elements on its board of directors—in effect a monopoly organization for overseas development and exploitation.[1]

Of nine directors on the board in 1930, five were on the AIC board in 1917 at the time of the Bolshevik Revolution: Matthew C. Brush, presi-

1. See Sutton, *Bolshevik Revolution,* op. cit.

dent and chairman of the executive committee of American International Corporation and director of the Empire Trust Company; Pierre S. Du Pont, member of the Du Pont family and a director of the Bankers Trust Company; Percy A. Rockefeller, of the Rockefeller family and director of National City Bank; Albert H. Wiggin, director of the Federal Reserve Bank of New York and the Rockefeller Chase National Bank; and Beekman Winthrop, of the Warburgs' International Banking Corporation and the National City Bank. Several prominent financiers joined the board of AIC during the 1920s, including Frank Altschul and Halstead G. Freeman of the Chase National Bank, Arthur Lehman of Lehman Brothers and the Manufacturers Trust Company, and John J. Raskob, vice president of Du Pont and director of General Motors and the Bankers Trust Company.

Mathew C. Brush, president, director, and chairman of the executive committee of American International Corporation and president of Allied Machinery, a subsidiary company, was also director and member of the executive committee of International Acceptance Bank (see Chapter 6), director and member of the executive committee of Barnsdall Corporation,[2] director of Empire Trust Company (120 Broadway) and Equitable Office Corporation (which owned and operated the building at 120 Broadway), director of Georgian Manganese Company,[3] and director and member of the Executive Committee of the Remington Arms Co., identified by General Butler in the last chapter. Matthew C. Brush was indeed in the vanguard of Wall Street.

Brush's political contributions, unlike those of other AIC directors, were apparently limited to $5000 to the campaign of Herbert Hoover in 1928. Brush was director of International Acceptance Bank, which profited from the inflation of the 1920s, as well as a director of Remington Arms (a suppressed name in the Butler Affair) while serving as president of American International, but appears to have been on the fringes of the occurrences explored in this book. On the other hand, four directors of American International have been identified as substantial financial supporters of Franklin D. Roosevelt: Frank Altschul, Pierre S. Du Pont, Arthur Lehman, and John J. Raskob between 1928 and 1932. The Lehman family and John J. Raskob were, as we have seen, at the very heart of Roosevelt's support. It is significant that AIC, the key vehicle for American participation in the Bolshevik Revolu-

2. Barnsdall Corporation was the company that in 1921 entered the Soviet Union to reopen the Caucasian oil fields for the Soviets and so enabled the Soviet Union to generate the foreign exchange required to develop a Sovietized Russia; see Sutton, *Western Technology and Soviet Economic Development,* 1917 to 1930 (Stanford: Hoover Institution, 1968), Vol. 1.
3. Ibid.

tion, should also be unearthed, even in an incidental form, in a study of the Roosevelt era.

THE BUTLER AFFAIR AND 120 BROADWAY

Testimony to the House Un-American Activities Committee on the attempt to convert the Roosevelt administration into a dictatorship with Major General Butler in a key role as Secretary of General Affairs had several links to 120 Broadway. There were at least half a dozen persons whom the committee should have subpoenaed to investigate the statements made under oath by General Butler, Captain Glazier, and Paul French; of these, four were located in, or had a significant connection with, 120 Broadway.

According to accused plotter Gerald MacGuire, the original meeting of the alleged participants was held in 1926 at the Bankers Club, 120 Broadway. The following extract from the committee hearings, records MacGuire's statement; the questioner was Chairman McCormack:

QUESTION. How long have you known Clark?
ANSWER. Well, I believe I said that I have done business with him and known him since 1925 or 1926.
QUESTION. Did he ever give you that kind of money before to use, as you say—in the way that he wanted you to represent him in these transactions?
ANSWER. In what transactions?
QUESTION. In those money transactions, since that time?
ANSWER. In what money transactions?
QUESTION. What I mean is this, since 1926, at the time that you met him and after; this was really the first time that you got this money without any receipt or papers or anything at all?
ANSWER. Yes.
QUESTION. And this dinner was at the Bankers Club, at 120 Broadway, wasn't it?
ANSWER. Yes.
QUESTION. Who was that dinner given to; was it given to anybody specially?
ANSWER. It was a regular luncheon.
QUESTION. Who was present at your table?
ANSWER. Mr. Christmas.
QUESTION. And yourself?
ANSWER. Yes.
QUESTION. And Mr. Clark?
ANSWER. Yes.[4]

4. House of Representatives, *Investigation of Nazi Propaganda Activities and Investigation of Certain Other Propaganda Activities*, Hearings No. 73-D.C.-6, op. cit., p. 80. "Mr. Clark" was Robert Sterling Clark and "Mr. Christmas" was Clark's attorney.

Thus, although the original meeting that brought together Robert S. Clark, his attorney Christmas, and bond salesman Gerald MacGuire was held at 120 Broadway, and Christmas and Clark were linked in numerous ways to MacGuire, neither Christmas nor Clark were called by the committee. Further, Captain Samuel Glazier of the CCC Camp at Elkridge, Maryland reported to the committee that Jackson Martindell had inquired about the training of 500,000 civilian soliders for political purposes. Martindell was not called by the committee to challenge or confirm the testimony implicating him in the Butler Affair.

The Du Pont Company, cited in the suppressed portion of the testimony, was located at 120 Broadway. Hugh S. Johnson, named by General Butler as a probable participant, had been located at 120 Broadway when working as research assistant to Baruch; Baruch's office was at the same address.[5] Clark, MacGuire, and Grayson M-P. Murphy had offices just down the street from No. 120; Clark at 11 Wall Street and MacGuire and Murphy at 52 Broadway.

It is also significant that names suppressed by the committee were located at 120 Broadway: the Du Pont Company executive office and Du Pont subsidiary Remington Arms. The other named participants, MacGuire, Clark, Christmas, Martindell, Grayson M-P. Murphy (at Rockefeller headquarters, 25 Broadway) were all located within a few blocks of 120 Broadway and within the previously described golden circle.

FRANKLIN D. ROOSEVELT AND 120 BROADWAY

We have noted that FDR's preferred office—he had two in the early 1920s—was the one at 120 Broadway. FDR's Georgia Warm Springs Foundation, Inc. was formed as a Delaware company in July 1926 with offices at 120 Broadway and remained at that address at least through 1936. The 1934 annual report for Georgia Warm Springs Foundation shows that its president was listed as Franklin D. Roosevelt, The White House, Washington D.C., with the head office of the foundation shown at 120 Broadway. The vice president and assistant secretary was Raymond H. Taylor, with secretary-treasurer Basil O'Connor, both shown at the 120 Broadway address.

Basil O'Connor was a close associate and business partner of Franklin D. Roosevelt. Born in 1892, O'Connor received his law degree from Harvard in 1915 and then joined the New York law firm of Cravath and

---

5. United States Senate, *Digest of Data From the Files of a Special Committee to Investigate Lobbying Activities*, 74th Congress, Second Session, Part I: List of Contributions, (Washington, 1936), p. 3.

Henderson for one year, leaving to work with Streeter & Holmes in Boston for three years. In 1919 Basil O'Connor established a law practice in New York under his own name. In 1925 the firm of Roosevelt and O'Connor was created, lasting until FDR's inauguration in 1933. After 1934, O'Connor was senior partner in O'Connor & Farber and in 1944 succeeded Norman H. Davis as chairman of the American Red Cross.

O'Connor was a director of several companies: in the 1920s, of New England Fuel Oil Corp., in the 1940s of the American Reserve Insurance Co. and the West Indies Sugar Corp. From 1928 until his death he was responsible for administration of the Georgia Warm Springs Foundation.

The Roosevelt New Deal was a gold mine to some of FDR's associates, including Basil O'Connor. Globe & Rutgers was an insurance company recapitalized with government funds, and the reorganization proved a rich source of fees for attorneys handling the liquidation and reorganization. Of these attorneys President Roosevelt's former firm of O'Connor & Farber demanded the largest single fee until Jesse Jones of the Reconstruction Finance Corporation cut it down. Here is a letter Jesse Jones wrote to Earle Bailie of J. & W. Seligman & Company about these fees:

October 6, 1934

Dear Mr. Bailie:
Our board is unwilling to invest in or lend upon stock in an insurance company, if indeed we have the right to do so, that contemplates paying such lawyers' fees, reorganization or otherwise, as is proposed in the case of the Globe & Rutgers, which we understand from information to be:

Basil O'Connor	$200,000
Root, Clark, Buckner & Ballantine	165,000
Sullivan & Cromwell	95,000
Prentice & Townsend	50,000
Cravath, de Gersdorff, Swaine & Wood	37,500
Martin Conboy	35,000
Joseph V. McKee	25,000
Coudert Brothers	12,000

or a total of $619,500. Even the suggested reduction to a total of $426,000 would be very much more than what would appear to this Corporation to be proper fees to be paid by an insurance company that is being recapitalized with Government funds.

Yours very truly,
JESSE J. JONES

Under court orders Mr. O'Connor's firm was paid $100,000 in 1934 and $35,000 more the following year.[6]

6. Jesse H. Jones, *Fifty Billion Dollars* pp. 209-210.

CONCLUSIONS ABOUT 120 BROADWAY

It is virtually impossible to develop an unshakable conclusion about the significance of 120 Broadway; explanations can range from conspiracy to coincidence.

What can we prove with direct, rather than circumstantial, evidence?

First, we know that U.S. assistance to the Bolshevik Revolution originated in the Wall Street golden circle in 1917 and was heavily concentrated at this particular address. Second, when FDR entered the business world in 1921, one of the two FDR offices was at this address, as was his law partnership with Basil O'Connor, and the Georgia Warm Springs Foundation. Third, Bernard Baruch and his assistant Hugh Johnson, later part of the planning and administration of the National Industry Recovery Act, were in the same building. NRA was a logical sequel to the trade associations of the 1920s, and FDR had a prominent role, along with Herbert Hoover, in the implementation of trade association agreements in the 1920s. Fourth, there was an association between General Electric and the Bolshevik Revolution, at least in building up the early Soviet Union. Executive offices of G.E. were at this address, as were those of Gerard Swope, the president of G.E. who authored the Swope plan.

Finally, the bizarre Butler affair had a few links with 120 Broadway. For example, this was Du Pont's New York address, although Remington Arms was at Rockefeller headquarters, 25 Broadway. Most of the plotters had other addresses, but still all within the golden circle.

Nothing is proven by a common geographical location. While 120 Broadway was a massive building, it was by no means the largest in New York City. But how does one explain the concentration of so many links to so many important historical events at one address? One *could* argue that birds of a feather flock together. On the other hand, it is more than plausible that these Wall Streeters were following the maxim laid down by Frederick Howe and found it more convenient, or perhaps more efficient for their purposes, to be at a single address. The point to hold in mind is that no other such geographical concentration exists and, if we ignore the persons and firms at 120 Broadway, there is no case for any relationship between these historical events and Wall Street. Which, incidentally, is also an excellent reason for retaining one's perspective in accepting the fact that we are discussing a small fraction of the banking community, a fraction that has in effect betrayed the financial center of a free economy.

CHAPTER 12

FDR and the Corporate Socialists

> At the first meeting of the Cabinet after the President took office in 1933, the financier and adviser to Roosevelt, Bernard Baruch, and Baruch's friend General Hugh Johnson, who was to become the head of the National Recovery Administration, came in with a copy of a book by Gentile, the Italian Fascist theoretician, for each member of the Cabinet, and we all read it with great care.
>
> *Mrs. Frances Perkins, Secretary of Labor under FDR.*

It is worth recalling at this point the epigraph to Chapter 1, that Franklin D. Roosevelt privately believed that the U.S. government was owned by a financial élite. There is, of course, nothing notably original about this observation: it was commonplace in the 19th century. In modern times, it has been averred by such dissimilar writers as Robert Welch and William Domhoff that America is controlled by a financial elite based in New York. The Soviets, who are not always altogether inaccurate, have used this theme in their propaganda for decades, and it was a Marxist theme before Lenin came along.[1]

---

1. It may be superfluous to record this literature, but for the sake of completeness and the benefit of the innocent reader, a few titles may be included: William Domhoff, *Who Rules America?* (Englewood Cliffs, N.J.: Prentice-Hall, 1967); Ferdinand Lundberg, *The Rich and the Superrich* (New York: Lyle Stuart, 1968), and Gary Allen, *None Dare Call It Conspiracy* (Seal Beach, Calif.: Concord Press, 1972).

It was under Roosevelt that quaint Keynesian notions—the modern versions of John Laws' con game with paper money—were introduced to Washington, and so the seeds of our present economic chaos were laid in the early 1930s under Roosevelt. Contemporary double digit inflation, a bankrupt Social Security system, bumbling state bureaucracy, rising unemployment—all this and more can be traced to Franklin Delano Roosevelt and his legislative whirlwind.

But while we now pay the price for these unsound and irresponsible policies, so pervasive is prevailing misinformation that even the identity of the originators of Roosevelt's New Deal and their reasons have been forgotten. While our economists cover their blackboards with meaningless static equations, a dynamic looting operation of the economy has been in progress by the authentic formulators of the liberal New Deal. While the bleeding heart social engineers have screamed at capitalism as the cause of the world's misery, they have been blissfully unaware that their *own* social formulas in part emanated from—and have certainly been quietly subsidized by—these same so-called capitalists. The tunnel vision of our academic world is hard to beat and equalled only by their avarice for a piece of the action.

What we do find is that government intervention into the economy is the root of our present problems; that a Wall Street cotérie has substantive, if subtle, muscle within this government structure to obtain legislation beneficial to itself; and that a prime example of this self-seeking legislation to establish legal monopoly under big business control was FDR's New Deal and, in particular, the National Recovery Administration.

The name Franklin Delano Roosevelt should suggest, but rarely does, a link with Wall Street. Both Delano and Roosevelt are prominent names in the history of American financial institutions.

Who was Franklin Delano Roosevelt?

Roosevelt's prepolitical career can be described only as that of financier. Both his family and career before 1928 and his election as Governor of New York were in the business world, more specifically the financial world. Between 1921 and 1928 Roosevelt was a director of 11 corporations headquartered in the Wall Street golden circle and president of a major trade association, The American Construction Council.

Certainly, if sheer weight of printed paper has any influence, the power of any financial élite should have collapsed long ago. The establishment does appear to have considerable endurance, but nowhere near as much influence as many believe. The most important leg sustaining the credibility and so the power of the élite is the academic community. This group has, in large part, swapped truth and integrity for a piece of the political power and the financial action. Apparently academics can be bought—and you don't have to pay overly much!

171

Furthermore, Roosevelt was not only president of United European Investors, Ltd., formed to take pecuniary advantage of the misery of German hyperinflation, but was one of the organizers of American Investigation Corporation, a high-powered financial syndicate. Roosevelts formed the financial firm Roosevelt & Son in the late 18th century, and Delanos operated in the financial arena from at least the mid-19th century. Roosevelts and Delanos may not have reaped the great wealth of Morgans and Rockefellers, but they were known and respected names in the halls of international finance. Even in the 1920s we find Uncle Frederic Delano on the Federal Reserve Board, and George Emlen Roosevelt as a director of Guaranty Trust, the *bête noire* of the Street if there ever was one.

It is also reliably recorded that Theodore Roosevelt's Progressive Party, the first step to the modern welfare-warfare state, was financed by the J.P. Morgan interests; consequently, it should not surprise us to find Wall Street backing Roosevelt in 1928, 1930, and 1932.

In brief, we have shown that Roosevelt was a Wall Streeter, descended from prominent Wall Street families and backed financially by Wall Street. The policies implemented by the Roosevelt régime were precisely those required by the world of international finance. It should not be news to us that international bankers influence policy. What appears to have been neglected in the history of the Roosevelt era is that, not only did FDR reflect their objectives, but was more inclined to do so than the so-called reactionary Herbert Hoover. In fact, Hoover lost in 1932 because, in his own words, he was unwilling to accept the Swope Plan, alias NRA, which he termed, not incorrectly, "a fascist measure."

We cannot say that Wall Streeter Roosevelt was always a highly ethical promoter in his financial flotations. Buyers of his promotions lost money, and substantial money, as the following brief table based on the data presented suggests:

How Investors Fared With FDR at the Helm

Company Associated with FDR	Issue Price of Stock	Subsequent Price History
United European Investors, Ltd.	10,000 marks (about $13)	Company wound up, stock-holders offered $7.50
International Germanic Trust Company, Inc.	$170	Went to $257 in 1928, liquidated in 1930 at $19 a share

Loss of stockholders' funds, however, can be an accident or mismanagement. Many honest financiers have stumbled. However, association with persons of known ill repute such as Roberts and Gould in United European Investors, Ltd. was not accidental.

FDR's association with the American Construction Council brings to mind Adam Smith's *obita dicta* that the law ". . . cannot hinder people of the same trade from sometimes assembling together, but it ought to do nothing to facilitate such assemblies, much less to render them necessary."[2] Why not? Because the American Construction Council was in the interests of the construction industry, not in those of the consumer of construction services.

The New York bonding business was made to order for FDR. As vice president of the Fidelity & Deposit Company of Maryland, FDR knew precisely how to operate in the world of politicized business, where price and product quality in the market place are replaced by "Whom do you know?" and "What are your politics?"

The United European Investors caper was an attempt to take advantage of the misery of German 1921-23 hyperinflation. The firm operated under a Canadian charter, no doubt because Canadian registration requirements were more lenient at that time. The most conspicuous observation concerns FDR's associates at U.E.I., including John von Berenberg Gossler, a HAPAG codirector of German Chancellor Cuno, who was responsible for the inflation! Then there was William Schall, FDR's New York associate, who had only a few years earlier been involved with German espionage in the United States—at 120 Broadway. The Roberts-Gould element in United European Investors was under criminal investigation; FDR *knew* they were under investigation, but continued his business associations.

Then we found that the background of the New Deal was speckled with prominent financiers. The economic recovery part of the New Deal was a creation of Wall Street—specifically Bernard Baruch and Gerard Swope of General Electric—in the form of the Swope Plan. So in Chapter 5 we expanded upon the idea of the politicization of business and formulated the thesis of corporate socialism: that the political way of running an economy is more attractive to big business because it avoids the rigors and the imposed efficiency of a market system. Further, through business control or influence in regulatory agencies and the police power of the state, the political system is an effective way to gain a monopoly, and a legal monopoly *always* leads to wealth. Consequently, Wall Street is intensely interested in the political arena

2. Adam Smith, *An Inquiry Into the Nature and Causes of the Wealth of Nations* (London: George Routledge n.d.), p. 102.

and supports those political candidates able to maximize the amount of political decision-making under whatever label and minimize the degree to which economic decisions in society are made in the market place. In brief, Wall Street has a vested interest in politics because through politics it can make society go to work for Wall Street. It can also thus avoid the penalties and risks of the market place.

We examined an early version of this idea: Clinton Roosevelt's planned society, published in 1841. We then briefly discussed Bernard Baruch's 1917 economic dictatorship and his declared intent to follow the course of a planned economy in peacetime and traced Baruch and his economic assistant Hugh Johnson to the very core of the National Recovery Administration. Some attention was then given to the Federal Reserve System as the most prominent example of private legal monopoly and to the role of the Warburgs through the International Acceptance Bank and the manner in which the bank was able to get society to go to work for Wall Street. In a final look at the years before FDR's New Deal we reviewed the operation of the American Construction Council, a trade association, the concept of which originated with Herbert Hoover, but with FDR as its president. The council had, as its stated objectives, limitation of production and regulation of industry, a euphemism for industry control for maximization of its own profits.

Then we examined the financial contributions of the 1928, 1930, and 1932 elections on the ground that such contributions are a very accurate measure of political inclinations. In 1928, an extraordinary percentage of the larger contributions, those over $25,000, came from Wall Street's golden circle. Such large sums are important because their contributors are more than likely to be identifiable after the election when they ask favors in return for their earlier subsidies. We found that no less than 78.83 per cent of the over $1000 contributions to the Al Smith for President campaign came from a one-mile circle centered on 120 Broadway. Similarly 51.4 per cent, a lesser but still significant figure, of Hoover's contributions came from within this same area. Then we demonstrated that, after his election, Herbert Hoover was given an ultimatum by Wall Street: either accept the Swope Plan (the NRA) or the money and influence of Wall Street would go to FDR who was willing to sponsor that scheme. To his eternal credit, Herbert Hoover refused to introduce such planning on the ground that it was equivalent to Mussolini's fascist state. FDR was not so fussy.

In FDR's 1930 campaign for Governor of New York, we identified a major Wall Street influence. There was an extraordinary flow of funds via the County Trust Company, and John J. Raskob of Du Pont and General Motors emerged as Chairman of the Democratic Campaign Committee and a power behind the scenes in the election of FDR.

Seventy-eight per cent of the pre-convention "early-bird" contributions for FDR's 1932 Presidential bid came from Wall Street.

The Swope Plan was a scheme to force American industry into compulsory trade associations and provide exemption from the anti-trust laws. It was baited with a massive welfare carrot to quiet the misgivings of labor and other groups. The administrator of the National Recovery Administration, which developed from the Swope Plan, was Baruch's assistant, General Hugh Johnson. The three musketeers, Johnson's circle of assistants, comprised Gerard Swope of General Electric, Walter Teagle, of Standard Oil of New Jersey, and Louis Kirstein of Filene's of Boston. Adherence to the NRA codes was compulsory for all firms with more than 50 employees. The Swope NRA Plan was greeted favorably by such socialists as Norman Thomas, whose main objection was only that they, the orthodox socialists, were not to run the plan.

Fortunately, NRA failed. Big business attempted to oppress the little man. The codes were riddled with abuses and inconsistencies. It was put out of its misery by the Supreme Court in the Schechter Poultry decision of 1935, although its failure was evident long before the Supreme Court decision. Because of failure of NRA, the so-called 1934 Butler Affair becomes of peculiar interest. According to General Smedley Butler's testimony to Congress, supported by independent witnesses, there was a plan to install a dictator in the White House. President Roosevelt was to be kicked upstairs and a new General Secretary—General Butler was offered the post—was to take over the economy on behalf of Wall Street. Far-fetched as this accusation may seem, we can isolate three major statements of fact:

1. There was independent confirmation of General Butler's statements and in some measure unwilling confirmation by one of the plotters.

2. There existed a motive for Wall Street to initiate such a desperate gamble: the NRA-Swope proposal was foundering.

3. The alleged identity of the men behind the scenes is the same as those identified in the Bolshevik Revolution and in the political promotion of FDR.

Unfortunately, and to its lasting shame, Congress suppressed the core of the Butler testimony. Further, The New York Times first reported the story fairly, but then buried and distorted its coverage, even to the extent of incomplete indexing. We are left with the definite possibility that failure of the Baruch-Swope-Johnson NRA plan was to be followed by a more covert, coercive take-over of American industry. This occurrence deserves the fullest attention that unbiased scholars can bring to it. Obviously, the full story has yet to emerge.

Once again, as in the earlier volume, we found a remarkable concentration of persons, firms and events at a single address—120 Broadway, New York City. This was FDR's office address as president of Fidelity & Deposit Company. It was Bernard Baruch's address and the address of Gerard Swope. The three main promoters of the National Recovery Administration—FDR, Baruch, and Swope—were located at the same address through the 1920s. Most disturbing of all, it was found that the original meeting for the Butler Affair was held in 1926 at the Bankers Club, also located at 120 Broadway.

No explanation is yet offered for this remarkable concentration of talent and ideas at a single address. Quite obviously, it is an observation that must be accounted for sooner or later. We also found a concentration of directors of American International Corporation, the vehicle for Wall Street involvement in the Bolshevik revolution, and heavy contributors to the Roosevelt campaign.

Can we look at this story in any wider perspective? The ideas behind the Roosevelt New Deal were not really those of Wall Street; they actually go back to Roman times. From 49 to 44 B.C. Julius Caesar had his new deal public works projects; in 91 A.D. Domitian had his equivalent of the American Construction Council to stop overproduction. The ultimate fall of Rome reflected all the elements we recognize today: extravagant government spending, rapid inflation, and a crushing taxation, all coupled with totalitarian state regulation.[3]

Under Woodrow Wilson Wall Street achieved a central banking monopoly, the Federal Reserve System. The significance of the International Acceptance Bank, controlled by the financial establishment in Wall Street, was that the Federal Reserve banks used the police power of the state to create for themselves a perpetual money-making machine: the ability to create money with a stroke of a pen or the push of a computer key. The Warburgs, key figures in the International Acceptance Bank—an overseas money-making machine—were advisers to the Roosevelt administration and its monetary policies. Gold was declared a "barbaric relic," opening the way to worthless paper money in the United States. In 1975, as we go to press, the fiat inconvertible dollar is obviously on the way to ultimate depreciation.

Did Wall Street recognize the result of removing gold as backing for currency? Of course it did! Witness Paul Warburg to a Congressional Committee:

Abandonment of the gold standard means wildly fluctuating foreign exchanges and, therefore, the destruction of the free inflow of foreign capi-

3. H. J. Haskell, *The New Deal in Old Rome:* How Government in the Ancient World Tried to Deal with Modern Problems (New York: Knopf, 1947), pp. 239-40.

tal and business. Weak countries will repudiate—or, to use the more polite expression, "fund their debts"—but there will be no general demonetization of gold. Gold at the end of the war will not be worth less but more.[4]

The inevitable conclusion forced upon us by the evidence is that there may indeed exist a financial élite, as pointed out by Franklin D. Roosevelt, and that the objective of this élite is monopoly acquisition of wealth. We have termed this élite advocates of corporate socialism. It thrives on the political process, and it would fade away if it were exposed to the activity of a free market. The great paradox is that the influential world socialist movement, which views itself as an enemy of this élite, is in fact the generator of precisely that politicization of economic activity that keeps the monopoly in power and that its great hero, Franklin D. Roosevelt, was its self-admitted instrument.

4. United States Senate, Hearings, *Munitions Industry*, Part 25, op. cit., p. 8105.

Appendix A   The Swope Plan

1. All industrial and commercial companies (including subsidiaries) with 50 or more employees, and doing an interstate business, may form a trade association which shall be under the supervision of a federal body referred to later.

2. These trade associations may outline trade practices, business ethics, methods of standard accounting and cost practice, standard forms of balance sheet and earnings statement, etc., and may collect and distribute information on volume of business transacted, inventories of merchandise on hand, simplification and standardization of products, stabilization of prices, and all matters which may arise from time to time relating to the growth and development of industry and commerce in order to promote stabilization of employment and give the best service to the public. Much of this sort of exchange of information and data is already being carried on by trade associations now in existence. A great deal more valuable work of this character is possible.

3. The public interest shall be protected by the supervision of companies and trade associations by the Federal Trade Commission or by a bureau of the Department of Commerce or by some federal supervisory body specially constituted.

4. All companies within the scope of this plan shall be required to adopt standard accounting and cost systems and standardized forms of balance sheet and earnings statement. These systems and forms may differ for the different industries, but will follow a uniform plan for each industry as adopted by the trade association and approved by the federal supervisory body.

5. All companies with participants or stockholders numbering 25 or more, and living in more than one state, shall send to its participants or stockholders and to the supervisory body at least once each quarter a statement of their business and earnings in the prescribed form. At least once each year they shall send to the participants or stockholders and to the supervisory body a complete balance sheet and earnings statement in the prescribed form. In this way the owners will be kept informed of the conditions of the business in such detail that there may be no criticism of irregularity or infrequency of statements or methods of presentation.

6. The federal supervisory body shall cooperate with the Internal Revenue Department and the trade associations in developing for each industry standardized forms of balance sheet and income statement, depending upon the character of the business, for the purpose of reconciling methods of reporting assets and income with the basis of values and income calculated for federal tax purposes.

7. All of the companies of the character described herein may immediately adopt the provisions of this plan but shall be required to do so within 3 years unless the time is extended by the federal supervisory body. Similar companies formed after the plan becomes effective may come in at once but shall be required to come in before the expiration of 3 years from the date of their organization unless the time is extended by the federal supervisory body.

8. For the protection of employees, the following plans shall be adopted by all of these companies:

(A) A WORKMEN'S COMPENSATION ACT, which is part of the legislation necessary under this plan, shall, after careful study, be modeled after the best features of the laws which have been enacted by the several states.

(B) LIFE AND DISABILITY INSURANCE. All employees of companies included in this plan may, after two years' service with such companies, and shall, before the expiration of five years of service, be covered by life and disability insurance.

(1) The form of policy shall be determined by the association of which the Company is a member and approved by the federal supervisory body. The policy will belong to the employee and

may be retained by him and kept in full force when he changes his employment or otherwise discontinues particular service as outlined later.

(2) The face value of a policy shall be for an amount approximately equal to one year's pay, but not more than $5,000, with the exception that the employee may, if he desires, increase at his own cost the amount of insurance carried, subject to the approval of the Board of Administrators, later defined.

(3) The cost of this life and disability insurance shall be paid one-half by the employee and one-half by the company for which he works, with the following exception: the company's cost shall be determined on the basis of premiums at actual age of employees less than 35 years old and on the basis of 35 years of age for all employees 35 or over and shall be a face value of approximately one-half a year's pay but limited to a maximum premium for $2,500 of insurance. An employee taking out insurance at age 35 or over will pay the excess premium over the amount based upon age 35. This will remove the necessity for restriction against engaging employees or transferring them from one company to another because of advanced age, as it will place no undue burden of high premiums upon the company.

(4) The life and disability insurance may be carried by a life insurance company selected by the trade association and approved by the federal supervisory body or may be carried by a company organized by the trade association and approved by the federal supervisory body, or a single company may be formed to serve all associations.

(5) The administration of the insurance plan for each company shall be under the direction of a Board of Administrators consisting of representatives, one-half elected by the employee members. The powers and duties of the Board for each company will be to formulate general rules relating to eligibility of employees, etc., but such rules shall be in consonance with the general plan laid down by the General Board of Administration of the trade association of which the company is a member, and approved by the federal supervisory body.

(6) Provision for the continuation of a policy after an employee leaves one company and goes to another in the same association, or goes to a company in another trade association; continuance of the policy after retirement on pension; provisions with regard to beneficiaries; total or partial disability; method of payment of premiums by payroll deductions or otherwise, weekly, monthly

or annually, shall be embodied in the plan formulated by the trade association, with the approval of the federal supervisory body.

(7) If an employee leaves a company to go with one which is not a member of the trade association; if he engages in business for himself; or if he withdraws from industrial or commercial occupation, he may elect to retain the portion of the policy for which he has paid, in whole, or in part, by the continued payment of the proportional full premium costs, or he may receive a paid up policy, or be paid the cash surrender value for the part for which he has been paying the premiums. The cash surrender value of that portion of the policy paid for by the company will be paid to the company which paid the premiums.

(C) PENSIONS. All employees of companies included in this plan shall be covered by old age pension plans which will be adopted by the trade associations and approved by the federal supervisory body. The principal provisions will be as follows:

(1) All employees may, after two years of service with a company coming within the scope of this plan, and shall, before the expiration of five years of service, be covered by the old age pension plan.

(2) All employees after two years' service may, and after five years' service shall be required to, put aside a minimum of one per cent of earnings, but not more than $50 per year, for the pension fund. The employee may, if he desires, put aside a larger amount, subject to the approval of the Board of Administrators.

(3) The Company shall be required to put aside an amount equal to the minimum stated above, namely one per cent of earnings of employees, but not more than $50 per year per employee.

(4) The above minimum percentage shall be the same for all employees who are less than 35 years of age when payments begin and the minimum percentage for these employees shall remain the same thereafter. The percentage to be set aside by employees coming into the pension plan at 35 years of age or over shall be so determined that it will provide a retiring allowance at age 70 the same as though they had begun one per cent payments at the age of 35. These provisions enable employees to go from one company to another in the same association or to different associations at any age with provision for retiring allowances which will be not less than the minimum rate of an employee who entered the pension plan at age 35.

(5) The amounts set aside by the employee and the company with

interest compounded semiannually at five per cent until retirement at age 70, for a typical average employee, would provide an annuity of approximately one-half pay.

(6) The administration of the pension plan for each company shall be under the direction of a Board of Administrators, consisting of representatives, one-half appointed by the management and one-half elected by the employee members. The powers and duties of the Board for each company will be to formulate general rules relating to eligibility of employees, conditions of retirement, etc., but such rules shall be in consonance with the general plan laid down by the General Board of Administration of the trade association of which the company is a member, and approved by the federal supervisory body.

(7) The amounts collected from the employees and the companies shall be placed with the pension trust organized by the association, the management of which shall be under the direction of the General Board of Administration referred to hereafter. In no case shall such funds be left under the control of an individual company.

(8) The Pension trust shall invest all funds and place them to the credit of the individual employees, including the income earned by the trust. If an employee goes from one company to another in the same association, the funds accumulated to his credit shall be continued to his credit with proper record of transfer. If an employee goes to a company in another association, the funds accumulated to his credit shall be transferred to his credit in the pension trust of the association to which he goes. If an employee goes to a company which does not come under these provisions or which is not a member of a trade association; goes into business for himself; or withdraws from an industrial or commercial occupation, the amount of his payments plus the interest at the average rate earned by the funds shall be given to him. If an employee dies before reaching retirement age, his beneficiary will receive the amount of his payments plus interest at the average rate earned by the funds. When an employee reaches retirement age, the entire amount accumulated to his credit, including his own payments and those of the company, plus accumulated interest, will be given to him in the form of an annuity. If an employee goes to a company which does not come under these provisions or which is not a member of a trade association; goes into business for himself; or withdraws from industrial or commercial occupation, he may elect to let the amount to his credit (namely, his own payments plus those of the company and the

accumulated interest) remain with the pension trust for transfer, if he should return to the employ of any company coming within the provisions of this plan. If he does not return to the employ of a company coming under these provisions, he may at any time thereafter withdraw the amount of his own payments plus interest at the average rate earned by the funds up to that time. Company contributions and accumulated interest credited to employees who die, or for reasons indicated above, receive or withdraw their own contributions and interest, shall be returned to the employer or employers who made the contributions.

(9) The rules governing the payments of pensions on retirement and all other rules governing its continuance shall be made by the trade association, approved by the federal supervisory body, and observed by the General Board of Administration and the Boards of Administration of the member companies.

(D) UNEMPLOYMENT INSURANCE. All employees on piece work, hourly work daily, weekly, or monthly work, with normal pay of $5,000 per year or less (approximately $96.15 per week) shall be covered by unemployment insurance.

(1) All such employees may, after two years of service with a company coming within the provisions of this plan, and shall, after five years of service, be each required to put aside a minimum of one per cent of earnings, but not more than $50 per year for an unemployment insurance fund.

(2) The company shall be required to put aside an amount equal to that put aside by the employees, as set forth above, namely one per cent of the earnings of each employee, but not more than $50 per year for each such employee.

(3) If a company regularizes and guarantees employment for at least 50 per cent of the normal wage paid each year to such employees, the company assesment for employees covered by such guarantee need not be made, but the employees will pay in a minimum of one per cent of earnings, but not more than $50 per year, into a special fund for their own benefit.

If such an employee leaves the company, dies or retires on pension, the amount to his credit in the special fund plus interest at the average rate earned by the special fund, shall be given to him or to his beneficiaries or added to his pension.

(4) If a company so plans its work that it is able to reduce unemployment, when the amount of such company's credit in the normal unemployment fund is equal to but not less than 5 per cent of the normal annual earnings of the employees covered, the company may cease making payment to the fund. Employees' payments

will continue. The company will resume payments when its credit in the normal unemployment fund falls below 5 per cent of normal annual earnings of the employees covered.

(5) When the weekly payments made from the fund for unemployment benefits amount to 2 per cent or more of the average weekly earnings of participating employees, the company shall declare an unemployment emergency, and normal payments by the employees and the company shall cease. Thereafter all employees of the company (including the highest officers) receiving 50 per cent or more of their average full-time earnings shall pay 1 per cent of their current earnings to the unemployment fund. A similar amount shall be paid into the fund by the company. The unemployment emergency shall continue until normal conditions are restored, which shall be determined by the Board of Administrators of each company. Thereupon normal payments will be resumed.

(6) The main provisions for the distribution of the funds shall follow along these lines, unless modified by the Board of Administrators as set forth in Section D, paragraph 7 hereof. A certain small percentage of the normal payments of the employees and the company may be considered as available for helping participating employees in need. A larger percentage of such normal payments may be considered as available for loans to participating employees in amounts not exceeding $200 each, with or without interest as may be determined by the Board. The balance of the funds shall be available for unemployment payments. Unemployment payments shall begin after the first two weeks of unemployment and shall amount to approximately 50 per cent of the participating employee's average weekly or monthly earnings for full time, but in no case more than $20 per week. Such payments to individual employees shall continue for no longer than ten weeks in any twelve consecutive months unless extended by the Board. When a participating employee is working part-time because of lack of work and receiving less than 50 per cent of his average weekly or monthly earnings for full time, he shall be eligible for payments to be made from the fund, amounting to the difference between the amount he is receiving as wages from the company and the maximum he may be entitled to as outlined above.

(7) The custody and investment of funds and administration of the unemployment insurance plan for each company shall be under the direction of a Board of Administrators consisting of representatives, one-half appointed by the management and one-half

184

elected by the employee members. The powers and duties of the Board shall be to formulate general rules relating to eligibility of employees, the waiting period before benefits are paid, amounts of benefits and how long they shall continue in any year, whether loans shall be made in time of unemployment or need, whether a portion of the funds shall be placed at the disposal of the Board for relief from need arising from causes other than unemployment, etc., but such rules shall be in consonance with the general plan laid down by the General Board of Administration of the trade association of which the company is a member, and approved by the federal supervisory body.

(8) If an employee leaves the company and goes to work for another company coming within the provisions of this plan, the proportionate amount remaining of his normal contributions, plus interest at the average rate earned by the funds, shall be transferred to such company and to his credit. If he leaves for other reasons, dies or retires on pension, the proportionate amount remaining of his normal payment, plus interest at the average rate earned by the funds, shall be given to him, or to his beneficiary, or added to his pension. When such employee's credit is transferred to another company, or paid to the employee or to his beneficiary under this provision, an equal amount shall be paid to the cooperating company.

GENERAL ADMINISTRATION. Each trade association will form a General Board of Administration which shall consist of nine members, three to be elected or appointed by the association, three to be elected by the employees of the member companies, and three, representing the public, to be appointed by the federal supervisory body. The members of the General Board, except employee representatives, shall serve without compensation. The employee representatives shall be paid their regular rates of pay for time devoted to Board work, and all members shall be paid traveling expenses, all of which shall be borne by the trade association. The powers and duties of this General Board shall be to interpret the life and disability insurance, pension and unemployment insurance plans adopted by the trade association and approved by the federal supervisory body, supervise the individual company Boards of Administration, form and direct a pension trust for the custody, investment, and disbursements of the pension funds, and in general supervise and direct all activities connected with life and disability insurance, pension and unemployment insurance plans.

Appendix B
Sponsors of Plans Presented for Economic
Planning in the United States at April 1932.[1]

American Engineering Council, New York.
American Federation of Labor, Washington.
Associated General Contractors, Washington.
Charles A. Beard, New Milford, Conn.
Ralph Borsodi, author and economist, New York.
Chamber of Commerce of the United States, Washington.
Stuart Chase, author and economist, Labor Bureau, New York.
Wallace B. Donham, Dean, Harvard School of Business.
Fraternal Order of Eagles (Ludlow bill).
Jay Franklin, author, *The Forum*.
Guy Greer, economist, *The Outlook*.
Otto Kahn, banker, New York.
Senator Robert M. La Follette, U.S. Senate.
Lewis L. Lorwin, economist, Brookings Institute, Washington.
Paul M. Mazur, investment banker, New York.
McGraw-Hill Publishing Co., New York.
New England Council, Boston.
Progressive Conference (La Follette bill).
P. Redmond, economist, Schenectady, N.Y.
Sumner Slichter, economist and author, Madison Wis.
George Soule, editor, *The New Republic*.
C. R. Stevenson, of Stevenson, Jordan, and Harrison, New York.
Gerard Swope, president, General Electric Co.
Wisconsin Regional Plan, State Legislature, Madison, Wis.
National Civic Federation, New York.

1. List Compiled by U.S. Dept. of Commerce.

Selected Bibliography

Unpublished Sources
Franklin D. Roosevelt archives at Hyde Park, New York

Published Sources
Archer, Jules *The Plot to Seize the White House,* (New York: Hawthorn Books, 1973)

Baruch, Bernard M., *Baruch, The Public Years,* (New York: Holt, Rinehart and Winston, 1960)

Bennett, Edward W., *Germany and the Diplomacy of the Financial Crisis, 1931,* (Cambridge: Harvard University Press, 1962)

Bremer, Howard F., *Franklin Delano Roosevelt, 1882-1945,* (New York: Oceana Publications, Inc., 1971),

Burton, David H., *Theodore Roosevelt,* (New York: Twayne Publishers, Inc., 1972)

Davis, Kenneth S., *FDR, The Beckoning of Destiny 1882-1928, A History,* (New York: G.P. Putnam's Sons, 1971)

Dilling, Elizabeth, *The Roosevelt Red Record and Its Background,* (Illinois: by the Author, 1936)

Farley, James A., *Behind the Ballots, The Personal History of a Politician,* (New York: Harcourt, Brace and Company, 1938)

Filene, Edward A., *Successful Living in this Machine Age,* (New York: Simon and Schuster, 1932)

Filene, Edward A., *The Way Out, A Forecast of Coming Changes in American Business and Industry,* (New York: Doubleday, Page & Company, 1924)

Flynn, John T., *The Roosevelt Myth,* (New York: The Devin-Adair Company, 1948)

Freedman, Max, *Roosevelt and Frankfurter, Their Correspondence—1928-1945,* (Boston, Toronto: Little, Brown and Company, 1967)

Freidel, Frank, *Franklin D. Roosevelt, The Ordeal,* (Boston: Little, Brown and Company, 1952)

Hanfstaengl, Ernst, *Unheard Witness,* (New York: J.B. Lippincott Company, 1957)

Haskell, H.J., *The New Deal in Old Rome, How Government in the Ancient World Tried to Deal with Modern Problems* (New York: Alfred A. Knopf, 1947.)

Hoover, Herbert C., *Memoirs. The Great Depression, 1929-1941,* (New York: Macmillan Company, 1952), Vol. 3.

Howe, Frederic C., *The Confessions of a Monopolist,* (Chicago: The Public Publishing Company, 1906)

Hughes, T.W., *Forty Years of Roosevelt,* (1944...T.W. Hughes)

Ickes, Harold L., Administrator, *National Planning Board Federal Emergency Administration of Public Works,* (Washington, D.C. Government Printing Office, 1934). Final Report 1933-34.

Johnson, Hugh S., *The Blue Eagle from Egg to Earth,* (New York: Doubleday, Doran & Company, Inc., 1935)

Josephson, Emanuel M., *Roosevelt's Communist Manifesto.* Incorporating a reprint of *Science of Government Founded on Natural Law,* by Clinton Roosevelt, (New York: Chedney Press, 1955)

Kahn, Otto H., *Of Many Things,* (New York: Boni & Liveright, 1926)

Kolko, Gabriel, *The Triumph of Conservatism, A Reinterpretation of American History,* (London: Collier-Macmillan Limited, 1963)

Kuczynski, Robert P., *Bankers' Profits from German Loans,* (Washington, D.C.: The Brookings Institution, 1932)

Laidler, Harry W., *Concentration of Control in American Industry,* (New York: Thomas Y. Crowell Company, 1931)

Lane, Rose Wilder, *The Making of Herbert Hoover,* (New York: The Century Co., 1920)

Leuchtenburg, William E., *Franklin D. Roosevelt and the New Deal 1932-1940,* (New York, Evanston, and London: Harper & Row, 1963)

Moley, Raymond, *The First New Deal* (New York: Harcourt Brace & World, Inc., n.d.)

Nixon, Edgar B., Editor, *Franklin D. Roosevelt and Foreign Affairs,* (Cambridge: The Belknap Press of Harvard University Press, 1969), Volume I: January 1933–February 1934. Franklin D. Roosevelt Library. Hyde Park, New York.

Overacker, Louise, *Money in Elections,* (New York: The Macmillan Company, 1932)

Pecora, Ferdinand, *Wall Street Under Oath, The Story of our Modern Money Changers,* (New York: Augustus M. Kelley Publishers, 1968)

Peel, Roy V., and Donnelly, Thomas C., *The 1928 Campaign An Analysis,* (New York: Richard R. Smith, Inc., 1931)

Roos, Charles Frederick, *NRA Economic Planning,* (Bloomington, Indiana: The Principia Press, Inc., 1937)

Roosevelt, Elliott and Brough, James, *An Untold Story, The Roosevelts of Hyde Park,* (New York: G.P. Putnam's Sons, 1973)

Roosevelt, Franklin D., *The Public Papers and Addresses of Franklin D. Roosevelt,* (New York: Random House, 1938), Volume One.

Roosevelt, Franklin D., *The Public Papers and Addresses of Franklin D. Roosevelt,* (New York: Random House, 1938), Vol. 4.

Schlesinger, Arthur M., Jr., *The Age of Roosevelt, The Crisis of the Old Order 1919-1933,* (Boston: Houghton Mifflin Company, 1957)

Seldes, George, *One Thousand Americans,* (New York: Boni & Gaer, 1947).

Spivak, John L. *A Man in His Time,* (New York: Horizon Press, 1967)

Stiles, Lela, *The Man Behind Roosevelt, The Story of Louis McHenry Howe,* (New York: The World Publishing Company, 1954)

United States Congress, House of Representatives. Special Committee on Un-American Activities. *Investigation of Nazi Propaganda Activities and Investigation of Certain Other Propaganda Activities.* Dec 29, 1934. (73rd Congress, 2nd session, Hearings No. 73-D. C.-6). (Washington, Government Printing Office; 1935)

United States Congress, Senate. Special committee to investigate lobbying activities. *List of contributions.* Report pursuant to S. Res. 165 and S. Res. 184. (74th Congress, 2d session). Washington, Government Printing Office, 1936)

United States Congress. Senate. Hearings before a subcommittee of the committee on military affairs. *Scientific and Technical Mobilization.* March 30, 1943. (78th Congress, 1st session. S. 702). Part 1. (Washington, Government Printing Office, 1943)

United States Congress. House of Representatives. Special Committee on Un-American activities (1934) *Investigation of Nazi and other propaganda,* (74th Congress, 1st session, Report No. 153) (Washington, Government Printing Office)

United States Congress. Senate, Hearings before the Committee on

Finance. *National Industrial Recovery.* S. 1712 and H.R. 5755, May 22, 26, 29, 31, and June 1, 1933. (73rd Congress, 1st session) (Washington, Government Printing Office, 1933)

United States Congress. Senate. Special committee investigating presidential campaign expenditures. *Presidential campaign expenditures.* Report pursuant to S. Res. 234, Feb 25 (calendar day, February 28), 1929. (70th Congress, 2nd session. Senate Rept. 2024). (Washington, Government Printing Office, 1929)

Warren, Harris, Gaylord, *Herbert Hoover and the Great Depression,* (New York: Oxford University Press, 1959)

Wolfskill, George, *The Revolt of the Conservatives, A History of The American Liberty League 1934-1940,* (Boston: Houghton Mifflin Company, 1962)

Index

192

193

194